TRANSACTIONS

of the

American Philosophical Society

Held at Philadelphia for Promoting Useful Knowledge

VOLUME 81 Part 2

The Massawomeck: Raiders and Traders into the Chesapeake Bay in the Seventeenth Century

James F. Pendergast

THE AMERICAN PHILOSOPHICAL SOCIETY

Independence Square, Philadelphia

1991

Library of Congress Catalog
Card Number 90-56111
International Standard Book Number 0-87169-812-9
US ISSN 0065-9746

TABLE OF CONTENTS

LIST OF FIGURES

ACKNOWLEDGMENTS

Several scholars have read and commented on one or another of the numerous drafts which have characterized this work over the past several years. In this regard I am grateful to Gordon Day, William Fenton, Elizabeth Tooker, Michael Foster, Bruce Trigger, Bernard Hoffman, and Conrad Heidenreich. I am indebted to Michael Foster for his linguistic assessment of the Massawomeck place names which I have related here. Norman Carlson, George Hamell, Dave Kohler, and Marvin T. Smith directed my attention to obscure references which I might otherwise have overlooked. Nevertheless, I hasten to explain that I retain full responsibility for the interpretations and opinions proffered here. I am indebted to Barry C. Kent, Richard J. McCracken, Charles L. Lucy and Dolores Elliott for making known to me the mysteries of late woodland archaeology in the Susquehanna River valley. I am grateful for Richard J. McCracken having commented on Chapter IV, n 8. Once again I thank my good neighbor Tom Manning who generously extended to me the use of his extensive library and in particular his library of Hakluyt Society publications. I appreciate the diligence of Wayne Poapst and Jill Eagle who put my manuscript on tape. Last, but always first, I thank Margaret for having read or listened to most of the innumerable drafts so that she too is now an "expert" on the Massawomeck.

I. INTRODUCTION

GENERAL

The Massawomeck are but one of several hinterland Indian groups which having made a brief, frequently violent, appearance during the seventeenth century, disappear. Eyewitness and contemporary accounts of the Massawomeck, which are confined to the period 1607–1634, are closely associated with the founding of the English Jamestown and Maryland colonies in tidewater Virginia. Unfortunately, references to the Massawomeck are brief and frequently apart from the mainstream of events. Often they are little more than asides, more tantalizing than revealing. Henry Fleet's *Journal* is a welcome exception, but his references to the Massawomeck are also peripheral to the main theme which recounts his experience as a fur trader on the Potomac River over the period 1627–1632. This paucity of primary and contemporary information has not prevented the accumulation of a sizable body of antiquarian and scholarly literature regarding the Massawomeck, much of it generated in the nineteenth century when there was a diligent, often multidisciplinary search for a Massawomeck identity which would classify them as one or another of the Iroquois tribes. Neither have twentieth century scholars let the matter rest.

Information regarding the Massawomeck is inextricably bound-up with the history, ethnohistory, and archaeology of the mid-Atlantic region and the Algonquians in the Chesapeake Bay region in particular. With the exception of William Fenton's work *Problems Arising from the Historic Northeastern Position of the Iroquois* (1940), Iroquoianists have neglected the Massawomeck. On the other hand, apart from Bernard Hoffman's work *Observations on Certain Ancient Tribes of the Northern Appalachian Province* (1964), tidewater Algonquian scholars, appear reluctant to investigate what nineteenth-century writers believed to be Iroquoians. It is against this background that I seek to expand upon what is known of the Massawomeck in the hope that it will be possible to enhance our understanding of trade between the mid-Atlantic Indians in the Chesapeake Bay latitudes and the Ontario Iroquois in the sixteenth century and the first three decades of the seventeenth century.

THE LITERATURE

Although the Cheseapeake Bay first appears on Juan Vespucci's map of 1526 as a result of the Giovanni da Verrazano and Estavão Gomes

1

voyages of 1524 and 1525 and the first account of Europeans being present there dates from prior to 1546, the Massawomeck are not mentioned, nor can they be identified, until 1607.[1] In December of that year John Smith, a charter member of the Jamestown Council, first learned of the Massawomeck from *Wahunsencawh*, principal chief of the Powhatan in whose territory the English had founded their Jamestown colony.

Smith records this first account of the Massawomeck in his *True Relation of such occurrences and accidents and noates both hapned in Virginia since the first planting of that Colony, which is now resident of the South part thereof, till the last returne from thence*. In reality this was a letter in which Smith recounts events which took place over the period from December 1606 to June 1608 to "a worshipfull friend" in England whose identity remains unknown. Upon its arrival in England in July 1608, Smith's letter aroused sufficient interest to warrant its being submitted for publication under this title on 13 August 1608. Since it was compiled before June 1608, references to the Massawomeck in Smith's *True Relation* are limited to his account of the information related to him by Powhatan while he was held his prisoner over the period December 1607–January 1608.

In 1612 Smith's second work, *A Map of Virginia with a Description of the Countrey, the Commodities, People, Government, and Religion*, was published. This work contains considerable information regarding the Indians of Virginia, but references to the Massawomeck are characteristically brief. It is the annex to Smith's work, which was also published in 1612, which concerns us here. Entitled *Whereunto is Annexed the proceedings of tho'e Colonies, since their first departure from England, with the discourses, Orations, and relations of the Salvages, and the accidents that befell them in all their Iournies and discoveries*, this annex contains several first-hand accounts by various Jamestown colonists. The relations by Doctor William Russell, Anas Todkill, and Nathaniel(l) Po(w)ell regarding Smith's encounter with the Massawomeck on Chesapeake Bay and with the *Tockwogh* and *Susquesahanock* who described the Massawomeck, all of which occurred in June and July 1608, are particularly germane to

---

[1] European interest in the latitudes of the Carolina Outer Banks and Chesapeake Bay in the sixteenth and seventeenth centuries in a large measure stemmed from the mistaken belief that in 1524 Giovanni da Verrazano had seen the Pacific Ocean when he had looked across the Outer Banks onto Albemarle and Pamlico sounds. This interpretation of Verrazano's discoveries is reflected in the pinch-waisted maps of North America prepared by Maggiolo in 1527 (Ganong 1964: fig. 34; Wroth 1970) and Verrazano's brother Gerolamo in 1529 (Quinn 1979 (1): fig. 44). As a result in the sixteenth century and well into the first quarter of the seventeenth, Spanish, French, and English explorers concentrated their search for a mid-Atlantic passage through America to the Orient in these latitudes. Some Jamestown settlers continued to search Chesapeake Bay tributaries for this passage westward as late as 1622 (Waterhouse 1622: 8-9). Nevertheless, until Smith first learned of the Massawomeck in 1607, there is no evidence that can be interpreted to be a reference to them by that name or any other.

this work. The invaluable map which accompanies Smith's *Map of Virginia* (Fig. 1) provides the orientation necessary to comprehend his and contemporary works regarding Jamestown and the surrounding region.

William Strachey[2] was not present in 1607 when Smith first learned of the Massawomeck from Powhatan nor was he present on the reconnaissances of Chesapeake Bay which took place during the summer of 1608 when Smith encountered the Massawomeck and then learned of their exploits from the Tockwogh Algonquians and Susquehannock Iroquoians at the head of Cheseapeake Bay. As a result, in the context of this work, Strachey's *Historie of Travell in Virginia Britania* (1612) is largely a paraphased repetition of Smith's works and the colonist's accounts set out in *The Proceedings*. Nevertheless, in his *First Booke of the First Decade* of his *Historie*, Strachey provides some new information regarding the Massawomeck which had not been recorded earlier.

In 1624 Smith published his *The General Historie of Virginia, New England and the Summer Isles with the names of Adventurers, Planters and Governours from the beginnings An: 1584 to the present 1624*. In this work Smith recapitulated and revised the information set out in his earlier works and *The Proceedings*. For example, he corrected the error included in both *True Relation* and *The Proceedings* regarding the homeland of the *Atquanahucke* which he had incorrectly located in the hinterland as a result of his having misinterpreted Powhatan's relation in 1607. Although there is nothing particularly revealing regarding the Massawomeck in Smith's *General Historie*, some texts have been expanded to elaborate on earlier descriptions which are germane to this work.

Few of the published administrative, private and diplomatic documents associated with the Jamestown colony refer to the Massawomeck. The known exceptions are the sometimes erroneous instructions provided for Sir Thomas Gates upon his being appointed governor of the colony in 1609, and the relation by Henry Spelman following his rescue by Samuel Argall in September 1610 after he had been held captive by the Powhatan and Potomac over the period 1609–1610.

Samuel Purchas published the first edition of *Purchas - his Pilgrimage* in 1613. It included a few extracts from Smith's *True Relation*, published

---

[2] William Strachey left England for Jamestown in the spring of 1609 with Sir Thomas Gates who had recently been appointed governor of the colony. Because their ship was wrecked on Bermuda in May 1609, Strachey did nor arrive in Jamestown until May 1610. After nearly sixteen months in the colony, during which time he served as secretary to the Jamestown Council, Strachey returned to England in 1612 with his manuscript *The Historie of Travell into Virginia Britania*. Unfortunately he arrived at the time when Smith's *Map of Virginia* and *The Proceedings* were ready to go to press. This conflict, in part, prevented Strachey's manuscript from being published then. It did not appear for 237 years, until 1849, when a manuscript copy of *The Historie* which Strachey had presented to Francis Bacon was published by the Hakluyt Society with R.H. Major as editor. In 1953 another copy of Strachey's manuscript, which Strachey had presented to Henry Percy, Earl of Northumberland, was published by the Hakluyt Society with Louis B. Wright and Virginia Freund as editors. The latter work has been followed here.

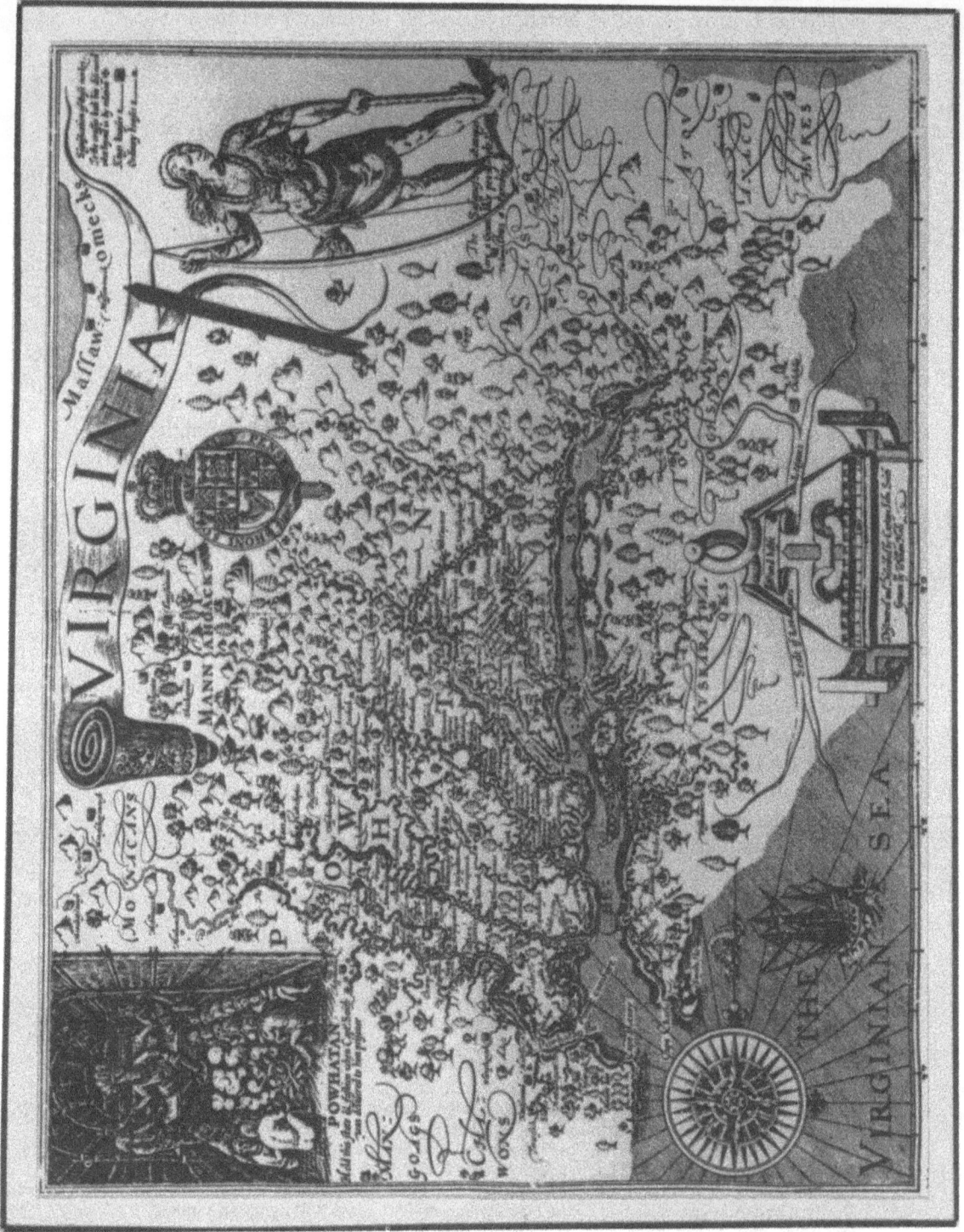

in 1608, and his *Map of Virginia* (1612). Purchas published the second
edition of *Pilgrimage* in 1614 with subsequent reprintings in 1617 and
1626. Between 1617 and 1621 Purchas commenced work on his enormous
work *Hakluytus Posthumus or Purchas - his Pilgrims* which appeared in
1625. In this work Purchas included the entire text of Smith's *Map of
Virginia* with a few minor changes. In 1624, Smith had published his
General Historie of Virginia in which he included a reprint of his *Map of
Virginia* as Book 2 and a rewrite of *The Proceedings* appeared as Book 3.
Barbour in his recent work *The Complete Works of Captain John Smith* (1986
(1): 126) provides a detailed comparison of the overlapping information
in the various Smith and Purchas texts.

However, it is Henry Fleet's *Journal*[3] of events on the Potomac over
the period 1627–1632 which provides the most detailed information regarding the Massomack or Massawomeck. During this period Henry
Fleet and his brother Edward traded furs with the Massawomeck, visited
their homeland, and heard accounts of their exploits from the Potomac
River Algonquians, however exaggerated they might be. While there
may be some confusion regarding the name of the ship from which Fleet
traded, there can be no doubt about the value of his *Journal* as an eyewitness account of Massawomeck activity on the Potomac River ca. 1632.

For the past two hundred years numerous scholars, popular authors,
and local historians have mined this literature to produce numerous
books, pamphlets, and papers regarding colonial Virginia and the Jamestown settlers. Seldom do the Massawomeck receive more than passing
mention in these works.

---

[3] Fleet's manuscript, *A Brief Journal of a Voyage in the Bark Virginia, to Virginia and other
parts of the Continent of America*, remained unpublished in the library of the Archbishop of
Canterbury at Lambeth Palace until 1876. At that time it appeared in Edward Neill's work
The Founders of Maryland as Portrayed in Manuscripts, Provincial Records and Early Documents
(Neill 1876). Apart from Hoffman's work *Observations on Certain Ancient Tribes* (1964), this
reference has not been used in connection with Massomack/Massawomeck research, although to this day, it remains the one of only two eyewitness accounts extant and in
many respects provides the most detailed accounts of these people when they were located
in the Appalachian hinterland.

II. PRIMARY ACCOUNTS, CONTEMPORARY LITERATURE, AND EARLY CARTOGRAPHY

MASSAWOMECK FIRST MENTIONED—DECEMBER 1607

John Smith first learned of the Massawomeck during the seven week period from December 1607 to January 1608 (Barbour 1986 (1): 9) when he was held captive by Powhatan. In his *True Relation* published in 1608 (Barbour 1969: 165–234), Smith relates how while held on the Pamunkey River by *Opechancanough* he met *Wahunsenacawh*, the principal chief of the Powhatan who was later known to the English as *Powhatan* (Wright and Freund 1953: 35 n. 1; Barbour 1969: 368, 472). At this time Powhatan related to Smith how, upon a sea beyond the hinterland *Quirank* mountains (Barbour 1969: 598), there dwelt " . . . a mightie nation called *Pocoughtronack* [Massawomeck], a fierce nation that did eate men and warred with the *Moyaoncer* [Piscataway] and *Pataromerke* [Potomac]" (ibid.: 186), both of which were located on the tidal reaches of the Potomac River. These Massawomeck made war " . . . upon all the world [so] that both coastal and foothill tribes regard them as mortal foes . . . " (Barbour 1986(2): 176; Schaeffer 1942: vi).

Undeterred by the fact that at the time he was being held prisoner by Powhatan, Smith assured Powhatan that " . . . when he [Smith] should find it convenient, wee should deliver under his sujection [Powhatan's] The Country of Manacam [sic][1] and Pocoughtraonack [sic] his enemies" (Barbour 1969: 192).

THE ZÚÑIGA MAP—CIRCA 1608 (Fig. 2)

As a result of having heard Powhatan's account of the Massawomeck in 1607, Smith included the following notation on the Pedro de Zúñiga map[2] on a hinterland body of water shown to be west of the Chesapeake

---

[1] The Monacan were eastern Siouians who in 1607 were located near the first falls on the James River, present day Richmond, Virginia (Swanton 1946: 152, 218).

[2] The "Zúñiga Map" should not be confused with Robert Tindall's 1607 map which is no longer extant nor with the 1608 copy of Tindall's map, known as the *Draughte of Virginia*, which is in the British Museum (Quinn 1979 (5): fig. 136; Cumming 1982: 279). Brown (1890 (1): 150), whose work has been criticized sharply by Barbour (1986), has suggested that Tindall's *Draughte of Virginia* was copied by Smith when he compiled his *Map of Virginia*. This opinion is shared by others (*Proceedings of the Massachusetts Historical Society*, 1925 Vol. 58; Mook 1943: 32). Recent scholars have suggested that the Zúñiga manuscript

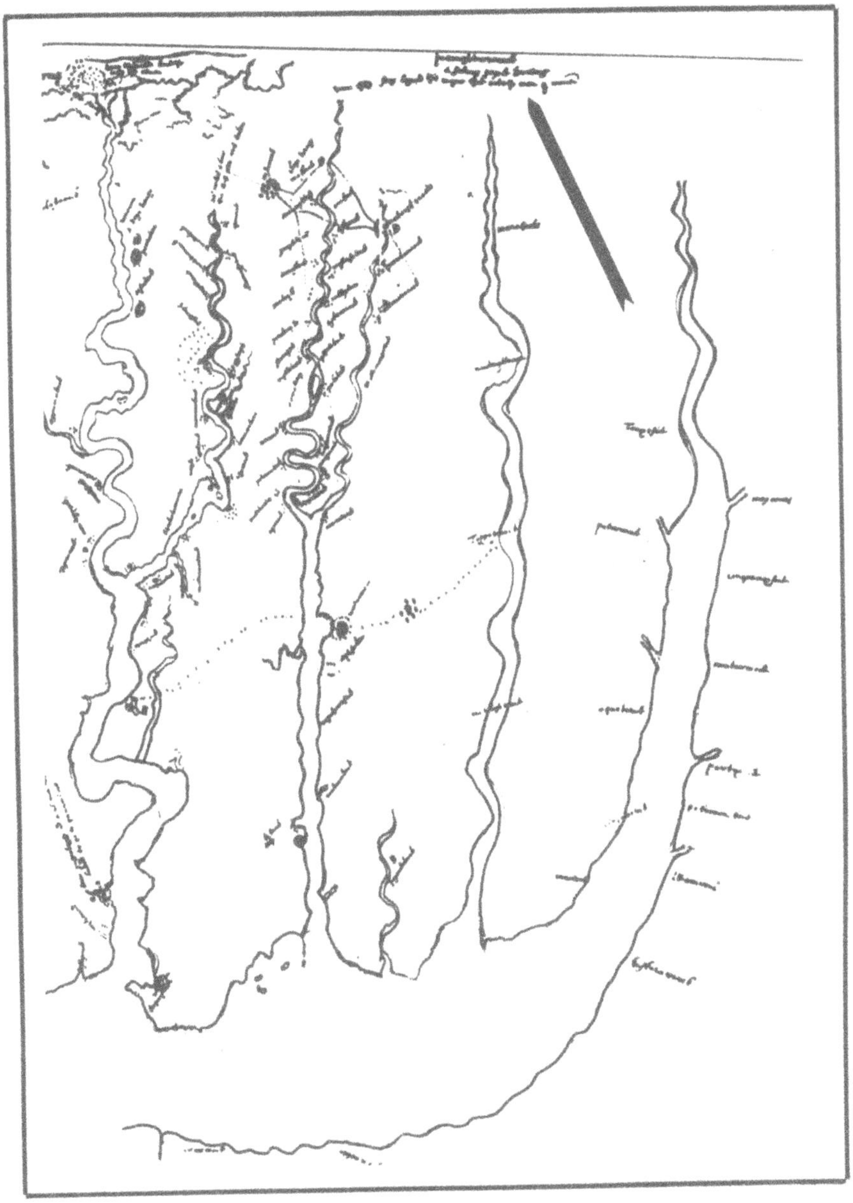

FIG. 2. A portion of the English map of 1608 sent to Spain by Pedro de Zúñiga. At the top is the note regarding the *'pocoughtawonauck'* (sic) or Massawomeck. North is on the right of the map.

---

map is Smith's sketch preliminary to his *Map of Virginia* and that Smith sent a copy of it to the "worshipfull friend" in England to whom he had sent the letter which was published in 1608 as the *True Relation*. Barbour (1969: 238-40) suggests that Smith may also have sent a copy of this same map to Henry Hudson. In any event, prior to September 1608 a copy of one of these maps was sent to the Spanish court by Don Pedro de Zúñiga, then the first Spanish ambassador to London after the defeat of the Armada in 1588. Later he was honored for his work with the title *Marques de Villa Flores and Avila*.

Bay at the headwaters of the Rappahannock River: "pocoughtawonauck / A Salvage people Dwelling / upon this seay beyond this mayne that eate men & women" (Barbour 1969: 238–40; McCary and Barka 1977: 14; Quinn 1979 (5): 488, fig. 13).

Robert Tindall's 1608 map *Draught of Virginia* (Mook 1943(b); Wright and Freund 1953: 31) which resembles the Zúñiga map does not extend into the hinterland sufficiently to depict the region in which the Zúñiga map locates the Pocoughtawonauck.

FIRST INDICATIONS ON CHESAPEAKE BAY—JUNE 1608

Jamestown colonists Walter Russell and Anas Todkill recount in *The Proceedings* (Barbour 1969: 399–405; Quinn 1979 (5): 319–21) how Smith set out on 2 June 1608 with a party of twelve colonists, including Russell and Todkill, to explore Chesapeake Bay in a barge. Crossing directly to Cape Charles on the east shore at the foot of the Bay, Smith made his way northward along the shore. In Tangier Sound, generally on the axis of the Kaskarawaocke (Nanticoke) River, Smith encountered the *Kaskarawaocke, Nause, Arsek* and *Nautaquake*. Algonquian bands who " . . . much extolled a great nation called Massawomeckes, in search of whom we returned [southward] by Limbo . . . ."[3] In his *General Historie* of 1624 Smith remarks that these bands on the eastern shore south of Tangier Sound were " . . . the best merchants of all other savages" (Lankford 1967: 61).

Having sustained injuries among his crew and had his boat damaged in a storm, Smith returned to the west side of Chesapeake Bay. When he reached *Kecoughtan*, the Powhatan village on Point Comfort at the mouth of the James River, Smith explained to the Indians that the injuries to the crew were the result of an encounter with the Massawomeck. News of this supposed engagement " . . . went faster up the [James] river than our barge . . . " as the Powhatan bands rejoiced at their having been joined by the English in their war against their mortal enemy, the Massawomeck (Barbour 1969: 405).

FIRST ENCOUNTER—JULY 1608

Nathaniel Po(w)ell and Anas Todkill, both Jamestown settlers who accompanied Smith on his second reconnaissance of the Bay, relate in *The Proceedings* how on 20 July Smith further ingratiated himself with the Powhatan by reporting to him that on his second reconnaissance

---

[3] Smith's "Limbo" and the "Straits of Limbo" were among the islands at the entrance to Tangier Sound, probably between Bloodsworth and Smith islands (Barbour 1969: 401). Earlier Stith (1747: 63) had located "Limbo" adjacent to Watts Island.

" . . . he went purposely to be revenged by the Massawomeck . . . ."
Two days later, having explored the Bolus (Patapsco) River upstream
six or seven miles from its mouth, Smith set out to cross to the east
shore of the Chesapeake Bay. There, east of present day Baltimore,
while crossing to the east side of the Bay, Smith met seven or eight
canoes of Massawomeck (Barbour 1969: 406; 1986 (2): 105, 109; Quinn
1979 (5): 322).

The Massawomeck prepared to attack Smith, but by resorting to the
ruse of placing many hats on sticks to give the impression of greater
strength, Smith caused them to withdraw. He followed them to the
shore anchoring his barge closeby, and eventually succeeded in enticing
two unarmed Massawomeck to approach his barge in a canoe. When
Smith presented each of them with a metal bell, the remainder of the
Massawomeck came aboard his barge readily. They gave Smith meat,
fish, bear-skins, bows and arrows, clubs, and shields, undoubtedly in
return for European goods although that is not stated in *The Proceedings*.
The remark by Poell and Todkill that the English " . . . understood them
nothing at all but by signs" (Barbour 1969: 407; Quinn 1979(5): 322) is
confirmed by Smith in his *General Historie* (1624: 24); " . . . we had a
conference by signs, for we understood one another scarcely." When
trading concluded at dusk, Smith fully expected the Massawomeck to
return and continue the exchange the next day, but in the morning they
were gone.

Both Smith's *Map of Virginia* (Barbour 1969: 361) and his *General Historie*
(1624: 33) were particular to observe the Massawomeck's " . . . desterite
[sic] in their small boats made of the barkes of trees sowed with barke
and well luted with gumme, [which] argueth that they are seated upon
some great water."[4]

THE TOCKWOGH ACCOUNT—JULY 1608

Having lost contact with the Massawomeck, Smith continued his reconnaissance of Chesapeake Bay, calling next on the Tockwogh Nanticoke Algonquian village at the head of the Bay which had within the
past few days been raided by the Massawomeck he had just met. This
village, which was in some manner not yet clear, associated with the
Delaware or Lenape nearby to the north (Brinton 1884: 139), is believed
to have been located on the Sassafras River near present day George-
town, Maryland (Barbour 1964: 216; Feest 1978(a): 241). *The Proceedings*

---

[4] Having been written before his second reconnaissance of Chesapeake Bay, Smith's
True Relation of 1608 makes no mention of this only encounter with the Massawomeck.
Smith's account of this event in his 1612 *Map of Virginia* is very brief (Barbour 1969: 361)
so the one by Powell and Todkill in *The Proceedings* is the most complete account of this
incident (Barbour 1969: 407). The Powell and Todkill account is the basis for Smith's in
his *General Historie* (1624: 33).

account by Poell and Todkill, both of whom were present, relates how when they first encountered the Tockwoghs they were well received, but upon seeing the Massawomeck material Smith had acquired, the Tockwogh became agitated. Once again Smith retold the tale of his having met and attacked the Massawomeck. Overjoyed by the news that the English had engaged their mortal enemy, the Tockwogh took Smith and his party to their village where they were entertained grandly. Smith learned that the "Many hatchets, knives and pieces of yron and brass" he saw in the Tockwogh village had been obtained from the *Susquesahanockes* (Susquehannock) a mighty people who too were mortal enemies of the Massawomeck. Upon learning that the Susquehannock were but two days beyond where his barge could ascend the Susquehanna River nearby, Smith prevailed upon the Tockwogh to take him to the mouth of the Susquehanna River. There he dispatched a Tockwogh party to bring the Susquehannock to meet him (Barbour 1969: 407; Quinn 1979 (5): 322). Kent (1984: 18,21) places the Washington Boro archaeological site in Lancaster County on the lower Susquehanna River in the time period ca. 1600–1625, making it contemporaneous with Smith's first encounter with the Susquehannock.

SUSQUE(SA)HANNOCK ACCOUNTS—JULY 1608

Sixty Susquehannock warriors responded to Smith's invitation, bringing him gifts which included venison, smoking pipes, baskets, shields, and bows and arrows. When weather prevented the whole Susquehannock party from returning to the Tockwogh village in their canoes, five Susquehannock chiefs readily came aboard Smith's boat and returned with him to the Tockwogh village, leaving the remainder of the Susquehannock party behind at the mouth of the Susquehanna River.

Poell and Todkill provide an eyewitness account of events in the Tockwogh village. The Susquehannock presented Smith with many gifts including skin clothing and chains of heavy marine shell beads. They stroked his body ceremonially in the traditionally Iroquoian greeting ritual all the while recounting to him tales of their enmity with the Massawomeck. They pledged him their assistance and allegiance and promised him gifts if he would " . . . stay with them to defend and revenge them to the Massawomecks." The English heard " . . . many descriptions and discourses they made us of *Atquanahucke, Massawomecke*, and other people, signifying they inhabit the river of Cannida [the St. Lawrence], and from the French to have their hatchets, and such tooles by trade . . ." (Barbour 1969: 408; Quinn 1979 (5): 323).

Here too Smith learned that the Susquehannock " . . knowe no more of the territories of Powhatan then [sic] his name, and he as little of them" (ibid.). In his account in *Map of Virginia* Smith simply states "These are scarce known to Powhatan" (Barbour 1969: 343). It is noteworthy that later in his *General Historie* (1624: 61) Smith elaborates, stating " . . . and he as little of them, *but the Atquanachuks are on the Ocean sea.*" This sets right Smith's error in his *Proceedings* regarding the hinterland marine location of the Atquanachuk which first arose as a result of his misinterpretation of Powhatan's relation in 1607. An examination of the Atquanachuk homeland as an indication of where Massawomeck territory was located in 1608 is set out at Appendix A.

In his 1612 *Map of Virginia* Smith does not mention his meeting with the Susquehannock in the Tockwogh village. However he does provide the following information: "Beyond the mountaines from which is the head of the river Patawomecke [Potomac], the Savages report inhabit their most mortall enemies, the Massawomeckes upon a great salt water, which by all likelyhood in either some part of Commada [Canada], some great lake, or some inlet of some sea that falleth into the South sea. These Massawomeckes are a great nation and very populous. For the heads of all those rivers, especially the Pattawomekes, the Pawtuxunts. The Sasquesahonocks, the Tockwoughes are continually tormented by them . . . " Barbour (1969: 361).

Smith repeats this information in his *General Historie* (1624: 33). However, Smith's *Map of Virginia* in his *General Historie* (Cumming et al. 1971: 281) does not include the hinterland in which the Massawomeck dwelt.

In September 1608, after Smith had heard the Tockwogh and Susquehannock accounts of the Massawomeck and before he published his *Map of Virginia* in 1612, Smith explained how Powhatan had corrected his (Smith's) misunderstanding of Powhatan's account of the Massawomeck homeland in 1607: "But for any salt water beyond the mountaines, the relations you have had from my people are false . . . " (Barbour 1969: 414; Quinn 1979 (5): 325). As a result it is surprising to find Smith stating erroneously again in 1612, in his *Map of Virginia*, that the Massawomeck lived " . . . upon a great *salt* water" (Barbour 1969: 361).

In the *Virginia* map which accompanies his work *Map of Virginia*, (Fig. 1) Smith shows the Massawomeck twice, once as *Massawomecks* and once as *Massawomeck*, presumably to differentiate between the tribe and its chief. He locates them on a large body of water in the hinterland beyond the headwaters of a tributary of the Potomac River, which appears to be a much enlarged and distorted representation of the Monocacy River, where his symbols for three "Kings houses" are shown.

Poell and Todkill recount how when Smith left the Susquehannock and Tockwogh at the head of Chesapeake Bay, he promised he would return the next summer to make war on their now common enemy. Later while making his way southward along the west shore of Chesapeake Bay, Smith met the Pawtuxunt (Patuxent) and Patawomecks (Potomac). These too he promised he would return the next summer to "revenge them of the Massawomeck." Smith explains in his *General Historie* (1624: 61) how at this time: "The highest mountains we saw Northward were called Peregrines mount, and a rocky river where the

Massawomeck went up, Willowbys River . . . the Susquehannocks river we called Smith's falls . . . Smals poynt is by the river Bolus."[5]

MANAHOAC ACCOUNT—AUGUST 1608

In his *General Historie* Smith (1624: 61–63) recounts how having left the Susquehannock and Tockwogh, he journeyed southward along the west shore of the Bay. In August 1608 he ascended the Rappahannock River to the first falls where a skirmish with the Manahoac took place. A Manahoac prisoner was questioned regarding the regions beyond the hinterland mountains generally, and the Massawomeck in particular.[6] When asked of the nations he knew, the prisoner mentioned the Powhatan and the Monacans and " . . . the Massawomeckes that were higher up in the mountain" than either of these tribes. When asked what was beyond the mountains, he replied capriciously, "the sun." He went on to explain that "The Massawomeckes did dwell upon a great water and had many boats and so many men that they made war with all the world."

INSTRUCTIONS TO SIR THOMAS GATES—1609

Sir Thomas Gates was appointed governor of Jamestown in the spring of 1609 but, having been shipwrecked in Bermuda, he was unable to take up his duties until May 1610. Although portions of his instructions regarding the conduct of his new duties (Barbour 1969: 262-8) are notorious for their "pompous mistakenness," the information they provide regarding the Massawomeck is pertinent. They explain that the "Massawomeckes make continual incursions uppon him [Powhatan] and uppon all those that inhabit the Rivers of Bolus and Mayomps[7] [the Patapsco and Potomac rivers] and to the northwest. Cocoughtuwonough [sic] infecteth him with Terrible warre . . . " (Bushnell 1907: 35).

HENRY SPELMAN'S RELATION—1609–1610

Henry Spelman, an English youth who had been held prisoner by Powhatan over the period 1609–1610, relates in his *Relation of Virginea* (Arber 1884: cxiv; Wright and Freund 1953: 46, 101; Hoffman 1964: 199;

---

[5] Wright and Freund (1953: 47) suggest that Smith's *River of Bolus* is the Gunpowder River while Barbour (1964: 204; 1969: 506) and Lankford (1967: 61) favor the Patapsco River. The Ralph Hall *Map of Virginia* of 1636 (Cumming et al. 1971: 283) indicates that it was the James River which was known as *Willowbyes Flu*.

[6] Thomson (1904: 503) and Bushnell (1935: 4) provide a full account of this incident.

[7] The river of the "Mayomps" refers to the Potomac River where the Piscataway village *Moyumpse* was located (vide Feest 1978: 250 for this Piscataway synonymy).

Barbour 1969: 5, 325, 462) how while a captive he: " . . . saw a Battell fought between the Potomeck and the Masomeck . . . Beings in the cuntry of the Potomeck the people of Masomeck weare brought tether in Canoes . . . in the forme of an Hoggs trought But sumwhat more hollowed in." Spelman goes on to describe how they conducted the battle with no great slaughter on either side before " . . . ye massomeckes having shott away most of their arrows and wantinge Vitall [food] weare glad to retier."

WILLIAM STRACHEY'S *HISTORIE*—1612

Strachey's *Historie* closely parallels accounts of the Massawomeck provided by Smith and the authors of *The Proceedings*. However, Strachey alters the *Pocoughtronack* mentioned by Powhatan to Smith in 1607 to read *Bocootawwonaukes* (Wright and Freund 1953:35, 132) and later to *Bocootawwonoukes* (ibid.: 36). His account of the Massawomeck canoes which were " . . . made of the Barkes of trees [probably elm] sowed togither and well luted with gum and rosyn of the Pine-tree argueth that they are seated upon some great water" (ibid.: 108) differs only slightly from Smith's account in his *Map of Virginia* (Barbour 1969: 361) and his *General Historie* (1624: 33).

Strachey's account of events in the Tockwogh village when Smith socialized with the Susquehannock and Tockwogh, which he did not witness, closely follows *The Proceedings* (Barbour 1969: 407–409; Quinn 1979 (5): 322–3). Although the following passage from Strachey's *Historie* is reminiscent of Smith's earlier accounts in his *Map of Virginia* (Barbour 1969: 361) and his *General Historie* (1624: 33) it does contain new information: "Beyond the Mountaines, from whence is the head of the River Pattawomeck [Potomac], do inhabit the Massawomecks (Powhatan's yet mortall Enemyes) upon a great salt that by all likelyhood may either be some part of Caneda, some great lake, or some Inlet of some Sea, that may fall into the West Ocean [Pacific], or Mar del zur[8] these Massawomecks are a great nation and very populous . . . " (Wright and Freund 1953: 107).

Strachey is paraphrasing the information set out by Smith in his *Map of Virginia* (Barbour 1969: 361) when he explains that: " . . . the Inhabitants of the heads of all those Rivers [on the west shore of Chesapeake Bay] expecially the Pattawomeckes the Pawtuxunts the Sasquesahanoughs the Tockwoghs are continually harrowed and frightened of them [the Massawomeck] . . . " (Wright and Freund 1953: 107).[9] Strachey also

---

[8] The "Mar del zur" is a sixteenth-century concept of a sea leading to Cathay which was associated with Sebastian Cabot's alleged voyage to the New World 1508-1509. (Quinn 1979 (1): 127).

[9] In his *Hakluytus Posthumus or Purchas-his-Pilgrims* Purchas quotes extensively from Smith's works (Barbour 1969: 324-25) but in this instance (1625 (18): 445) he follows Strachey's text.

repeats Smith's information that the region thirty leagues northward from the Patuxent River to the Susquehanna River, which includes the Bolus, or Patapsco, River region was uninhabited (Wright and Freund 1953: 47).

CAPTAIN HENRY FLEET, FUR TRADER—1622–1634

After the cluster of events described by the Jamestown settlers over the period 1607–1610, the Massawomeck are not mentioned again until Henry Fleet recounts in his *Journal* how he met them as fur traders on the Potomac River in 1632.[10]

---

[10] This is not the earliest evidence of English trading on the Potomac River. In 1613 Argall led a party of Jamestown settlers to the Potomac where, together with other business, he traded corn with the "non-beaver" Potowomeck (Brown 1890 (2): 641). This expedition is probably better known for having located bison in this region. In 1622 the settlers were on the Potomac again (Waterhouse 1622: 8-9). In 1623 Spelman led a Jamestown party to trade at tidewater on the Potomac. Henry Fleet, the twenty-four year old son of William Fleet who was a member of the Virginia Company of London, took part in this expedition. When they were attacked by the Anacostank, Spelman was killed and Fleet was taken prisoner (Scarf 1879: 14). Having incorrectly identified the Conoy Algonquian "Nacotchtank" band (Feest 1978: 250) as an Iroquoian group located on the Potomac some fifteen miles upstream from the Piscataway Conoy band, Merill (1979: 552) has erroneously placed Fleet in contact with *Iroquoians* at this time.

Upon his release by the Anacostank, Fleet returned to England where he joined William Clobery, a London merchant prepared to invest in the Virginia trade. In September 1627 Fleet returned to Virginia as master of the 100-ton *Paramour* hired by Clobery to trade for furs on Chesapeake Bay. This signaled the beginning of a regular and organized trade in furs on Chesapeake Bay. That year a shipload of furs was sent to Holland. It is also recorded that year that Robert Poole, a Jamestown settler, spent several weeks with the Patuxent trading blue glass beads which had been manufactured at Jamestown. Fleet's activities from 1627 to 1632 are not known in detail but it is clear that from 1627 to 1640 he was active in the Chesapeake fur trade. His account of trading with the Massawomeck at Great Falls on the Potomac in 1632 is the most detailed on these people and their homeland.

Over the period 1630-1631 William Clairbourne, an associate of Fleet's, established a fur trading post on Kent Island in Chesapeake Bay east of present day Annapolis, Maryland, and later a smaller post on Palmers Island in the mouth of the Susquehanna River. These posts were intended to provide access to the Patuxent on the western shore, who were said to be the best beaver trappers, and the beaver-rich Susquehannock who, as early as 1626, had been trading with the Dutch at New Amsterdam. Powhatans had been excluded from the trade after the rebellion of 1622. Fausz (1985, App. B: III) suggests these posts were also intended to discourage Iroquois interference from the north. The Massawomeck, in the Cumberland Gap region at this time, would not have been affected.

In 1633 so much cloth was diverted from the Virginia settlers to the fur trade, and so many skins were leaving the colony, much to the detriment of the colonists, that an act was passed to regulate the trade and protect the settlers interests.

Before Claibourne and his fellow Virginians could fully reap the lucrative returns anticipated from the posts on Kent and Palmers islands, the Marylanders, led by Leonard Calvert, arrived at the mouth of the Potomac River in March 1634 with Henry Fleet as their guide. Fleet and Calvert visited the Potowomeck on the Potomac to negotiate land for the settlers (Menard and Carr 1982: 171). Calvert has explained how in March 1634 the Marylanders had arrived too late to participate in the fur trade with the Massawomeck that year. Significantly Calvert also remarked how over the period 1629-1632 the Massawomeck had directed large quantities of furs to Kirke and the English at Quebec.

In May 1632, after being held captive by the Anacostank at the Great Falls on the Potomac River over the period 1623–1627 (Morrison 1921: 222), Fleet returned to the Potomac River to trade for beaver pelts. Upon entering the river he sent his brother Edward ahead to trade with the *Piscattoway* (Piscataway) who lived on the Piscataway River three days up the Potomac River. Henry planned to trade with the Potomack lower on the Potomac but finding few furs in that region, he moved farther up the river to a location near present day Washington D.C. to trade with the *Nacostines* (Anacostank) (Feest 1978: 250), his erstwhile captors. Relations between the Anacostank and the Piscataway were strained. Shortly before Fleet arrived the Massawomeck had killed some 1000 Piscataway to establish the Anacostank as the Massawomeck-approved middlemen who were " . . . to convey all such English truck [trade goods] as commeth into the river to the Massomacks . . . [and as a result the Anacostank were] protected by the Massomacks or *Cannyda Indians*" (Neill 1876: 25; Feest 1978: 243). Although the Piscataway were still a potent force and more numerous, they were reluctant to interfere overtly in these Anacostank middleman activities.

Fleet fortuitously encountered Daniel Gookin (1792), an English interpreter, who may have visited the Massawomeck homeland, and several Algonquians who had recently been there. From them he learned that the Massawomeck were a populous nation governed by four "kings" who lived in villages named *Tohoga, Mosticum, Shaunnetowa*, and *Usserahak*. As a result Fleet estimated they greatly outnumbered the 5000 tidewater Algonquians whom Smith believed to be living in the Potomac River region at that time.[11] Upon learning that the Massawomeck had accumulated a large stock of beaver skins for trade, Henry brushed aside Anacostank and Piscataway attempts to prevent him from dealing directly with the Massawomeck. On 14 June he sent Edward to bring the Massawomeck to trade with him at the Great Falls on the Potomac River.

Eleven days later, on 25 June, Henry set out to meet Edward on his return journey from *Tonhoga* (Tohoga?). Upon reaching the Great Falls Henry remarked that the country above the falls was " . . . rocky and mountainous like Cannida." While it is likely that Fleet was familiar with the Potomac region, there is no reason to believe that he had been to the region on the St. Lawrence River known to the French as "Canada," or to the "Cannyda" region.

On 3 July Edward appeared at Great Falls with two Massawomeck.

By 1638 the Marylanders had eclipsed the Virginians in the fur trade on Chesapeake Bay. Nevertheless the loyalty of the post on Kent Island remained in doubt for some time. Although the fur trade on Chesapeake Bay and the Potomac River continued on into the 1650s (Morrison 1921; Menard and Carr 1982: 190; Fausz 1985), there is no mention of the Massawomeck after Calvert's remarks in May 1634.

[11] In his 1612 *Map of Virginia* Smith estimated that within sixty miles of Jamestown there were some 5,000 Indians who were subject to Powhatan (Barbour 1969: 354).

He recounted to Henry how from the Great Falls he had spent seven days traveling to the Massawomeck homeland and five days on the return voyage. He also related how there he had visited thirty palisaded Massawomeck villages, one of which contained three hundred houses and how when he delivered four presents to the king of this village, the king had " . . . dispersed them to the rest" of the people, an act reminiscent of Iroquoian gift-giving which did not prevail among the tidewater Algonquians. Edward explained how 110 Massawomeck with "40,000 weight" of furs were on their way to trade at Great Falls. The two Massawomeck who had returned with Edward had been selected by the "nation" to confirm Fleet's ability to provide the European trade goods they would demand before they entered into a direct trading arrangement with him which would bypass their Anacostank middle-men. The Anacostank, fearful of losing their preferred status as mid-dlemen, regaled these Massawomeck scouts with tales alleging that Fleet meant to destroy them and steal their furs in retaliation for the recent Massawomeck attack on the Piscataway. When Fleet confronted the An-acostank with their treachery, they offered to ally themselves with him and promised, if he would give their king a present, that they would bring the Massawomeck to him for trade.

There matters stood until 10 July when six Massawomeck from *Us-serahak*, by their account a town of 7000, arrived ready to trade directly with Fleet. They drew a map of their country for Fleet and explained they had brought sixty canoes of furs, but these too had been intercepted by the Anacostank who still hoped to prevent the Massawomeck from trading directly with Fleet. "These [Usserahak Massawomeck] promised if I would show them my truck [they would] get a great store of canoes to come down with one thousand Indians that should trade with me . . . ." Fleet noted that the Usserahak " . . . delight in hatchets, and knives of large size, broad cloth, and coats, shirts and Scottish stockings. The women desire bells and some kind of beads" (Neill 1876: 30).

The following day " . . . there came from another place [not from the Massawomeck homeland] seven lusty men with strange attire; they had red fringe . . . . Their language was haughty and they seemed to ask me what I did there, and demanded to see my truck, which upon view, they scorned. They had two axes such as Captain Kirk traded in Can-nida . . . ." They went aboard Fleet's vessel and drew for him a map of their country which did not differ greatly from that which the Us-serahak Massawomeck had drawn for him earlier. Significantly Fleet states, "These [Indians] called themselves *Mosticums* [a Massawomeck 'nation'] but afterwards I found [from the Usserahak] they were of a people [who lived] three days journey from these [the Massawomeck of Mosticum] and were [in fact] called *Hereckeenes* who with their own beaver, and that which they get from those that do ajoin upon them do drive a trade in Cannida, at the plantation [settlement], which is fifteen days journey from this place"; presumably that was the distance of the "plantation" from the Hereckeenes homeland.

On 14 July one of Fleet's men, William Elderton, joined the Hereckeenes who pretended to be Mosticum Massawomecks to visit their homeland. The next day when the Usserahak Massawomeck learned what Elderton had done, they were agitated fearing that " . . . these people were not their friends, but that they were Hereckeenes," who would eat Elderton. When the Usserahak Massawomeck had finished trading with Fleet, they demonstrated their satisfaction with the direct trading arrangement telling Fleet that two hundred Massawomeck would soon come to Great Falls to trade beaver pelts with him.

On 18 July Fleet visited the Piscataways down river to excuse himself " . . . for trading with those that were [their] enemies . . . ," the Massawomecks. On 7 August, the Massawomeck from Tonhoga, the Tohogoes, arrived at Great Falls to trade saying they had come because " . . . they had received assurance to our [Fleet's] love of the Usserahaks, although the Nacostines [the Anacostank middlemen] had [still] much laboured the contrary." While trading was in progress the Tohogoes became alarmed when they learned that one of Fleet's men (Elderton?) had been " . . . slain by the Hireckeenes (sic) three days journey beyond them, and that they [the Hereckeenes] had beguiled us [Fleet] with the name Mostikums, one of their [Massawomeck] confederation nations. Nevertheless, they being desirous to have some trial [experience] of us, had sent us these skins . . . [and if Fleet's trading arrangements were satisfactory] they would come [from] all four nations [Tonhoga, Mosticum, Shaunetowa and Usserahak] and trade with . . . "Fleet (Neill 1876: 33).

When Fleet's trade goods were depleted he moved from Great Falls to *Moyumpse*, a Piscataway village farther down the Potomac River. He was followed into Piscataway territory, apparently with impunity and without fear of their recent enemies, by " . . . three cannibals of *Usserahak, Tohoga*, and *Mosticum* . . . [who said] they would come with a great number of people that should trade with us as formerly they had spoken . . . ." The magnitude of the fur trade of which Fleet was a part can be appreciated from the report that in 1632 some 2,700 pounds of fur worth 120 pounds sterling were collected by the Chesapeake Bay fur traders (Fausz 1985: 5).

Fleet returned to Jamestown where in September 1632 he was tried for having violated fur trade regulations. When he was cleared of these charges, he built a new barque of sixteen tons which he sent " . . . to the *Cannadies* [Massawomeck] with provisions and such merchandize . . . " (Neille 1876: 36). Unfortunately nothing more is known of this expedition.

CALVERT'S LETTER—1634

On 30 May 1634, Leonard Calvert, governor of the newly established Maryland colony at *St. Mary's* at the mouth of the Potomac River, wrote to Sir Richard Lechford his partner in England in the Maryland venture, reporting in part on the Marylander's participation in the Massawomecke fur trade (10): "Whilst we were a-doing these things [establishing St. Mary's City] our pinnace by our director followed the trade of beaver through all parts of the precincts of this province. But by reason of our late arrivall here [March 1634] we came too late for the first part of the trade this year; which is the reason I have sent hom so few furrs - (they being dealt for by those Virginians [Fleet and Claibourne?] before our crossing) - the second part of our trade is now in hand, and is like to prove very beneficiall. The nation we trade withal at this time a-year is called the Massawomeckes. This nation cometh seven eight and ten days journey to us - these are those from who Kircke had formerly all his trade of beaver. We have lost by our late comming 3000 skins, which other Virginians have traded for, but hereafter they shall come no more here, wherefore I make no doubt but next year we shall drive a very great trade if our supply of truck fail not" (*Maryland Historical Society Fund Publication* No. 35, 1899: 25–26; Morrison 1921: 224; Hoffman 1964: 200; Menard and Carr 1982: n25).

Calvert's account suggests that Fleet was still trading with the Massawomecks in 1634 and, presumably, he had done so in 1633 as well. This conclusion accords with what we know of Fleet's plans for his new sixteen-ton barque which he had dispatched to trade with the *Cannadies* in the spring of 1633.

In view of the importance of the Massawomeck fur traders to the Maryland settlers, it is surprising to find that they are not located on Lord Baltimore's map of 1635 *Nova Terrae-Mariae* (Cumming et al. 1971: 262; 1982: 288). Nor are they located on Ralph Smith's *Map of Virginia* of 1636 (ibid.: 283), the other English map of this period.

Calvert's letter of May 1634 is the last contemporary documentary evidence of the Massawomeck. Possibly conflict between Virginians and Marylanders had driven them from trading on Chesapeake Bay.

JOHANNES JANSSON MAP—1636

Johannes Jansson's map *America Septentrionale* of 1636 (Goss 1990b: 72), although largely derivative, is particularly significant in this context because it is the first map to place the Massawomeck in the hinterland immediately west of Chesapeake Bay. Theretofore Smith's manuscript map of 1608, the so-called *Zúñiga* map (Fig. 2), and his map *Virginia* of 1612 (Fig. 1), both place them in a marine or lacustrine location a considerable distance west of Chesapeake Bay in keeping with the information related by Smith in 1607 and by Powell and Todkill in 1608.

Jansson's map reflects their presence in a region adjacent to the Bay over the period 1632–1634 where they had ready access to Jamestown and Maryland fur traders as Henry Fleet and Leonard Calvert have related.

It is noteworthy that there was sufficient Dutch interest in the English fur trade on Chesapeake Bay in 1636 for them to record the presence of the Massawomeck who were the principal source of these furs. The absence of the Massawomeck from Jansson's map *Nova Anglia Novum Belgium et Virginia* (Goss 1990b: 70), which was also published in 1636, may reflect more recent information regarding the Massawomeck which, for some reason, would have them cease to be important in this fur trade. In this event the disappearance of the Massawomeck may be attributed to 1635, possibly 1636. Regrettably neither Blaeu's 1635 map *Nova Belgica et Anglio Nova* (Goss 1990a: 164), which is a copy of Adriaen Blockx's manuscript map *Carte Figurative* ca. 1614, nor his 1638 map *Viginial partis australis et Floridae partis orientalis* (Goss 1990b: 74), quite incorporate the region in which Jansson locates the Massawomeck in 1636.

DANIEL GOOKIN—ca. 1640

Daniel Gookin, an Irish contemporary of Fleet's who had been present in the Virginia colony from November 1621 to 1643 (Tyler 1901 (4): 170; (9): 234–35), did not add much to information in the *Proceedings* when he wrote: "There is a numerous race of Indians that live upon a great lake or sea. Some report it to be salt water while other fresh . . . . This people I conceive to be the same that Capt. Smith in his *History of Virginia* [sic] doth in several places call Massawomecks . . . . Now the place where he met with and heard of this great people of Massawomecks [sic] was at the head of Chesapeake Bay or Gulf - and he saith they had recourse thither from the lakes and seas where they lived, in canoes of bark and trees" (Anon; Gookin 1792).

This suggests that Gookin had not been to the Massawomeck homeland, although he had advised Fleet when he arrived on the Potomac River in 1632 that they held a large store of furs to trade. Presumably Gookin's Algonquian traveling companions were the source of his information regarding Massawomeck fur holdings.

THE ROBERT DUDLEY MAP—1647

Sir Robert Dudley's derivative map *Virginia Vecchio é Nuoua* of 1647 (Fig. 3) also locates the Massawomeck in the hinterland west of Chesapeake Bay. I have not been able to discern whether this information was simply copied from Jansson's map of 1636, or derived from Fleet's and Calvert's accounts.

FIG. 3. The Dudley Italianate derivative map of 1647. The *Massawomecks* are indicated in the hinterland between the Potomac and Susquehanna rivers on the headwaters of the Patapsco River.

THE JOHN FARRER MAP—1651

John Farrer's map *The Sea of China and the Indies* of 1651 (Fig. 4) is a derivative map, which is seldom used as evidence in this context. On this map (Cumming et al. 1971: 269) the word "Massawomeckes" appears in quite small letters in the mountainous region between the headquarters of the Delaware River and a greatly attenuated eastern tributary of the Potomac River. In this location Farrer's "Massawomeckes" are close to "A Mighty great Lake" and the "Canada Flu," The St. Lawrence River, both of which are shown on the Farrer map to be adjacent to, or part of, "Nova Francia." Although Farrer's map is later than Dudley's, Farrer appears to be still reflecting Smith's 1608 location of the Massawomeck on the River of Canada at a time when they were living in the Chesapeake Bay hinterland as related by Fleet and Calvert over the period 1632–1634.

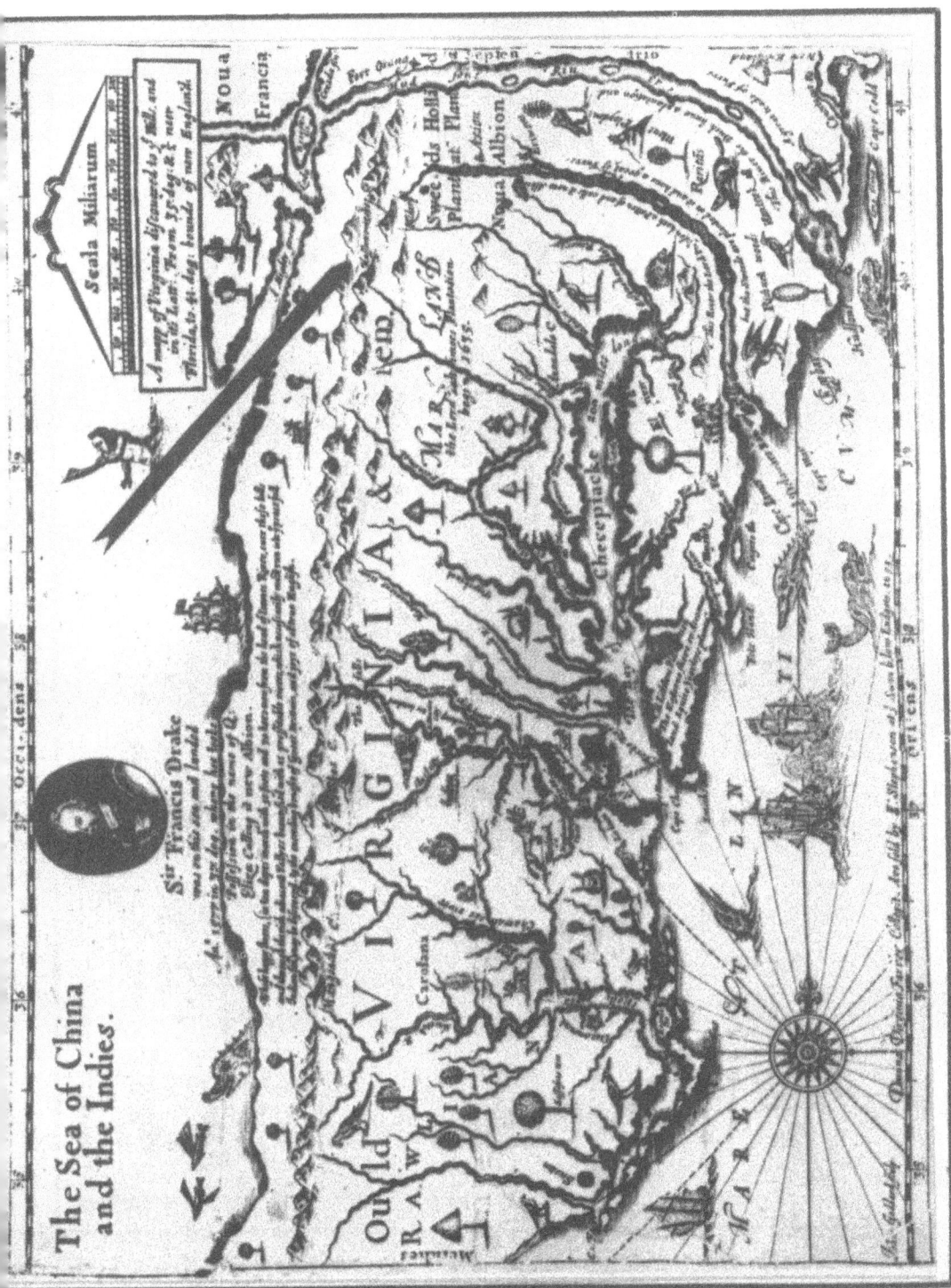

FIG. 4. The John Farrar map of 1651. The *Massawomeckes* (sic) appear in small print in the mountains indicated below the cartouche in the top right corner. North is on the right of the map.

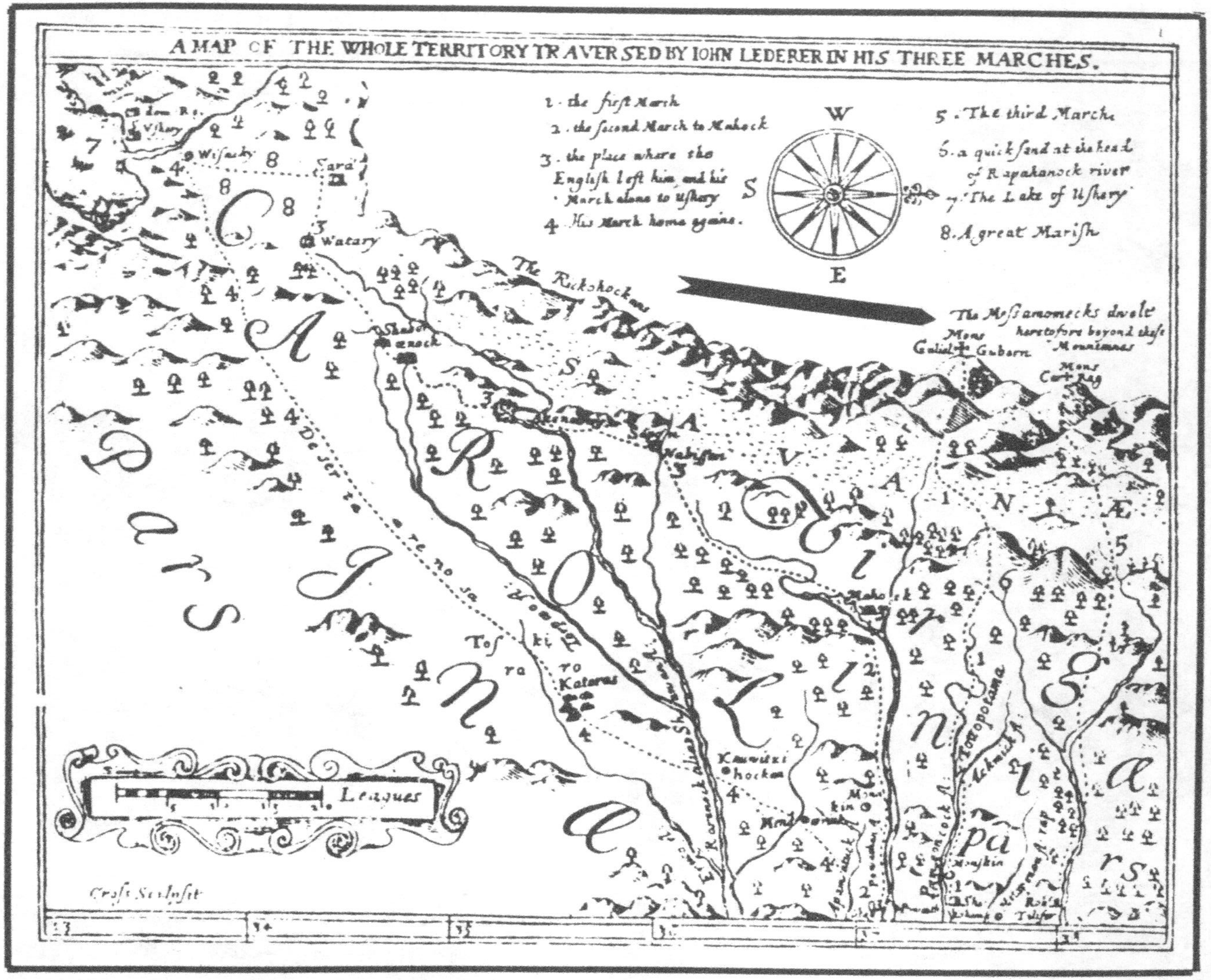

FIG. 5. The John Lederer map of 1672. The *Massawomecks* are indicated to have "dwelt heretofore beyond these mountains" on the right side of the map at the headwaters of the Potomac River. North is on the right of the map.

THE JOHN LEDERER MAP—1672

Although it is significantly later, the largely derivative Lederer map of 1672 (Fig. 5) also places the Massawomeck in a location that accords best with Smith's explanation of 1608 rather than the events in the period 1632–1634. Beyond the mountains at the headwaters of several rivers which drain into Chesapeake Bay on the west side, one of which has been identified as the James (Hoffman 1964: 205) in a blank area on the map there is the legend: "The Massawomecks dwelt/heretofore beyond these/Mountains." Lederer makes no mention of the Massawomeck in his text (Cumming and Right 1958). Apparently he too was not aware, as Dudley was, of the Virginia and Maryland fur trade with the Massawomeck.

THE DELISLE MAP—ca. 1700

This unpublished sketch map, which was probably compiled between 1700 and 1703 by Guillaume Delisle in the preparation for the 1703 map of America attributed to Father Claude Delisle, is particularly significant. In reality it is little more than a compilation of notes reflecting information derived, largely, from the Jesuit *Relations*. However, in the hills to the west of the head of Chesapeake Bay there is the legend: "Massawomeckies Savage people who are almost continually at war with the Susquehannock and the Tockwogh." Although this is simply a repetition of the information Smith revealed in 1608 which placed the Massawomeck on the River of Canada, Delisle's location of this legend in the hinterland west of Chesapeake Bay fits with the Fleet and Calvert accounts for the period 1632–1634. Delisle thereby provides the sole French reference to the movement of the Massawomeck from a lacustrine area associated with the River of Canada and the "Canyda region" to a place adjacent to, and west of, Chesapeake Bay where they engaged in a fur trade with the Virginians and Marylanders. Appearing more than sixty years later when the Massawomeck were no longer indicated on the maps of the day, Delisle's map reflects the Massawomecks' location indicated by Jansson in 1636 and Dudley in 1647.

These accounts which describe events in the period from prior to 1608 to ca. 1634, and the several seventeenth-century maps mentioned, comprise the known inventory of primary and contemporary documentary and cartographic sources regarding the Pocoughtronack, Massomack, and Massawomeck. Most are closely associated with English settlement and trading activities in the tidewater regions of Chesapeake Bay. Some are eyewitness accounts, but apart from Smith's brief encounter on Chesapeake Bay in 1608 and certain events described in Fleet's *Journal* for the period 1627–1632, much of the information is hearsay repetition of sometimes misunderstood relations by the Indians. Nevertheless, it does constitute the body of primary and contemporary evidence on which to premise our understanding of the Massawomeck.

III. THE CURRENT SITUATION

THE MASSAWOMECK HOMELAND

Many have long sought to identify the Massawomeck homeland. Possibly the first to do so was Thomas Jefferson who, being keenly interested in the Indians, noted in 1781 that: "Westward of all these tribes[1] beyond the mountains and extending to the great lakes, were the Massawomecs, a most powerful confederacy who harassed unremittingly the Powhatans and the Manahoacs" (Jefferson 1904: 497; Bozman 1837: 112–4; Thomson 1904; Peden 1955). In the nineteenth century several scholars suggested a location for the Massawomecks. General John S. Clark prepared a map[2] to illustrate Hawley's *Early Chapters in Cayuga History*, published by the Oneida Historical Society in 1879, which included the notation "Massawomecks Near Lake Erie. Described by Gov. Smith 1608." That same year Scarf (1879: 88) located the Massawomeck homeland on Lake Ontario. In 1892 Beauchamp (1892: 98) explained, " . . . there are good reasons for placing them [the Massawomeck] even south of the Eries. It is true that either the Seneca or the Eries could have gone down the Allegheny and reached the Potomac by a short portage."

Twentieth-century scholars too have sought to locate the Massawomeck homeland. Bushnell (1907: 35) placed the *Masawoymeles* and the *Coughtuwonough* (sic) to the north and northwest of the Potomac. Bushnell (1930, 1935, 1937) used Smith's 1612 *Virginia* map (Fig. 1) to locate some seventeen to nineteen Algonquian village sites on the Potomac River which were known to Smith. McCary and Barka (1977: 85) have suggested that by demonstrating Smith's accuracy, Bushnell has enhanced the credibility of his location of the Massawomeck on the "great water" in the hinterland. This seems unlikely. Smith was familiar with much of the Chesapeake Bay tidewater regions and sometimes beyond, but significantly he explains: " . . . as far as you see the little crosses [on his 1612 map] on rivers, mountains, and other places have been discovered; the rest was had by information of the Savages and are set down according to their instructions" (Barbour 1969: 344). The location of the Massawomeck indicated on the *Virginia* map is well beyond the

---

[1] Jefferson also mentions the *Monacans*, making them synonymous with the Tuscarora, and the *Monahoacs*.

[2] Winsor includes this map in his *Narrative and Critical History of America* (1884: 293) to illustrate Shea's essay *Jesuit, Recollects and the Indians*.

regions explored by Smith, and so cannot be considered as reliable as places within the bounds of Smith's explorations as McCary and Barka have suggested. However, this alone cannot serve to deny the accuracy of the information Smith obtained from the Indians for his *Virginia* map.

Hoffman (1964: 200–201) has sought to locate the Massawomeck homeland adjacent to Chesapeake Bay by coupling Governor Calvert's account of the Massawomeck traveling eight to ten days to trade at the Great Falls on the Potomac in 1634 with Edward Fleet's account of his seven day journey to Massawomeck homeland in 1632. As a result Hoffman suggests that Massawomeck territory was located on the headwaters of the Potomac River, or possibly beyond on the Youghiogheny branch of the Monongehela River which rises a scant 10 miles from the upper reaches of the Potomac River on the Pennsylvania-West Virginia border near the Cumberland Gap.

Hoffman has also examined closely the Massawomeck connection with the Erie (ibid.: 204).[3] He notes Ragueneau's explanation in 1648 that: "This Lake called Erie, was formerly inhabited on its Southern shores by certain tribes who we call the Nation of the Cat; they have been compelled to retire far inland to escape their enemies who are farther to the West" (Thwaites 1895–1901 (33): 63). In particular Hoffman notes the French concept of the Erie as reflected by the notation on the Bernou map ca. 1680 (Hoffman 1964: 206; White 1978: 408) below *Lac Teiocha rontiong du communement Lac Erie*, which reads: "This Lake is not Lake Erie as people usually call it. Erie is a part of Chesapeake Bay Virginia, where the Eries have always lived."

Following a detailed examination of the historic and archaeological

---

[3] Unfortunately very little is known of the Erie at this time, (White 1978 a). Archaeological data suggest that in the period 1535-1640 elements of the Erie occupied the lacustrine regions at the east end of Lake Erie and the hinterland along the banks of Cattauraugus Creek. Ethnohistory and history indicate that prior to 1644-1645 they were driven deep into the hinterland (White 1978a: 415). Gendron (1868: 8) stated in 1644 or 1645 that: "This lake called Erie was formerly inhabited on its southern shores by certain people whom we call the Nation of the Cat. . . This nation has been obliged to withdraw very far into the country to escape from their enemies who are toward the *west*" (emphasis mine). It has been suggested that this move occurred ca. 1638 under pressure from the western Iroquois, the Seneca and Cayuga, who had also caused the Wenro to move to Huronia at about the same time (Thwaites 1895-1901 (8): 302; (17): 25) Beauchamp (1889 (a): 125) believed that the Erie at one time, perhaps within the historic era, included the Seneca.

The orientation westward in the Gendron text must be a copying error probably caused by the similarity between the French for west, *ouest*, and east, *est*. An identical incontrovertible error appears in the Jesuit *Relation* for 1641 where "west" has crept into the text when "east" is essential to this account regarding the origin of the marine shell used by the Neutral.

Bernard Hoffman (1964: 234) has examined the extent of Erie territory and postulated a territory significantly larger than any heretofore recognized. It includes the headwaters of the Potomac and Monongahela rivers. Marion White (1971: 22; 1978: 412) has rejected this hypothesis largely on the basis that it encompasses too large an area and because it included several major watersheds which, she suggests, was not a normal Iroquoian practice.

literature, Hoffman concludes, in part, that the Massawomeck lived west
of the Piedmont Siouan tribes, " . . . on the headwaters of the Potomac
and on the upper Ohio drainage area" (ibid.: 222). On the basis of the
archaeological data he places them on the south shore of Lake Erie in
the region attributed to the Whittlesey people and at the headwaters of
the Mongahela and Youghiogheny rivers in the region attributed to the
Mongahela.

Barbour (1964) has suggested, in general terms, that the Massawomeck lived beyond the Nanticoke Algonquians without stating in which
direction. Merrill (1979: 552) places them initially " . . . on the headwaters of the Potomac and upper Ohio rivers" and later they
" . . . moved into the lower Potomac to settle." This latter location appears to be derived from his opinion that the Nacotchtank, Anacostank,
were Iroquoians. In his definitive work Barbour (1986 (2): 11, n. 2) has
noted how one edition of Smith's *General Historie* (1624), The Second
Book, includes the statement " . . . with the estate and condition of
eight other several nation adjoyning to them" which is not included in
all editions. As a result Barbour concludes that the Massawomeck did
not dwell in an area adjacent to Powhatan.

At present the Zúñiga map of 1608, Smith's *Virginia* map of 1612, the
Jansson map of 1636, the Dudley map of 1647, the Farrer map of 1651,
the Hondius-Visscher map of 1669, the Lederer map of 1672, and the
Delisle map of ca. 1700 are the only maps, French or English, which
locate the Pocoughtronack/Massawomeck/Massomack.

IDENTIFICATION OF THE MASSAWOMECK

Many have recorded their opinions regarding the identity of the Massawomeck. Most have sought to associate them with one or another of
the seventeenth-century Iroquoian tribes, frequently with one of the Five
Nation Iroquois. Thomas Jefferson (1904: 497) explained "These [the
Massawomeck] were probably the ancestors of tribes known at present
by the Six Nations." It is noteworthy that Jefferson's criticism of Stith's
work (1747: 67) *History of the First Discovery and Settlement of Virginia*, in
which he suggested that the Massawomeck were Seneca Iroquois, was
directed at the literary value of the work, not at matters of substance.
Unfortunately the original documents available to Stith had disappeared
by the time Rutman edited his work in 1969. Charles Thomson com-
menting on Jefferson's identification noted that the "Indians which lived
to the north of them [the Manhattan] between the Kittatinney mountains
or highlands and the Lake Ontario and who call themselves Mingoes
and are called by the French writers Iroquois, by the English Five Nations, and the Indians to the southward, with whom they are at war,
Massawomacs" (Thomson 1904: 503; Bozman 1837: 112–14). He also

noted that the "Monacans and their friends better known latterly as the Tuscarora, were probably connected with the Massawomecs, or five nations" (Thomson 1904: 498). In an appendix to Jefferson's *Notes on the State of Virginia* (1787), Thomson also suggested that the Massawomeck were the Five Nation Iroquois (Thomson 1904: Peden 1955; Weslager 1983: 35).

Nineteenth-century scholars were particularly diligent in their attempts to equate the Massawomeck with one of the better-known Indian groups. De Witt Clinton (1820: 40, 64) argued that the Massawomeck were Iroquois. Gallatin (1836 (2): 421) suggested that the Massawomeck encountered by Smith were a group of Iroquois fulfilling their career of conquest and, for him, the incident proved that the Iroquois were a great power who dominated a large region. Bozman (1837: 112–14) supported this identification, but Royce (1881: 179) did not accept this identification or this explanation. In 1844 Bancroft (1844 (1): 134) suggested they were Mohawks. Scarf (1879: 14) agreed, relating erroneously that Fleet had said he went to trade on the Potomac with Mohawk man-eaters. Miner (1845: 20) suggested that "some" of the Five Nations had " . . . come from the Wyoming valley where they were known as Massawomecks." He went on to explain that the Massawomeckes and the Massachusett derived their name from association with a hill, which in a case of the Massawomeck was a reference to the hills which surround the Wyoming valley. In his work *Notes on the Iroquois* Schoolcraft (1847: 155) noted how, under the name *Massawomeck*, the Iroquois dominated the "Powhattanic Confederacy" in Virginia. Later (1857: 180, 194) he repeated this Iroquois identification in his work *History of the Indian Tribes*. Several nineteenth-century scholars have supported Schoolcraft's identification (Scarf 1879: 88; Mooney 1894: 12–13; Fowke 1894: 72), and it has prevailed in this century (Tyler 1907; 88, n. 1; Cadzow 1936: 13; Barbour 1964: 215–16; Mouer 1983: 21).

Over a long period William Martin Beauchamp expressed several opinions regarding Massawomeck identity. In his *Origin and Early Life of the New York Iroquois*, a paper read before the Oneida Historical Society, 20 March 1886 (Beauchamp 1889 (a): 124), he noted that the "Early writers made these [Massawomeck] any part of the Five Nations, but later students have identified them, as in the case of the *Entouhonorons*, with both the Erie and the Senecas, these being firm friends until 1653." Having mentioned Fleet's fur trading in 1632, Beauchamp (ibid.) concludes again that " . . . there remains no doubt that this name [Massawomeck] included the Erie and Senecas, then or previously allied." Beauchamp (1889 (b): 121–25) repeated his conviction that in 1632 when they were encountered by Fleet, the Massawomeck were Eries and Senecas then, or earlier, allied, but it was as Seneca that " . . . the Massawomecks of New York made themselves feared by the Indians of Virginia." In 1892, he explained that the Massawomeck were clearly related to the Iroquois but were likely Erie which included more than one "nation" (1892: 98–99). He speculated that Edward Fleet may have reached the southern villages of the Erie in 1632 and that the four kings Fleet mentions may have been the four nations of the Erie (ibid.: 100–101). In 1894 he remarked, "The general description of the Massawomeckes points to a nation of this family [Iroquoian] to the south of the Eries, whereas they have been identified with the Five Nations without sufficient reason" (1894: 62). In 1895 he opined that, "It seems proper to consider the Massawomeck a southern division of a numerous group" which he believed to be elements, at least, or the Seneca and Erie (1895: 323). In 1898 he suggested that they " . . . were probably a southern offshoot of the Erie" (1898: 87) Later he raised the possibility that they might be Oneida (1900: 88). Finally in 1905 (1905: 193–94) Beauchamp concluded they were the Erie group who once had inhabited Cattaraugus and Chautauqua countries.

Tooker (1894: 185 n. 1) draws upon Strachey's revised spelling of Smith's *Pocoughtronack, Bocootawwonaukes* and later *Bocootawwnonoukes* (Wright and Freund 1953: 35, 132, 136), and the Zúñiga map, to interpret *Bocootaw* as "fire" and *anuak* as "people" and thereby connect Strachey's otherwise unknown *Bocootawwonoukes* with the *Atsistaehronons* or "Fire Nation" who were enemies of the Huron and Neutral (Thwaites 1895–1901 (21): 95; Goddard 1978: 668–72). Strachey compounds the problem when he identifies the *Pocoughtronack* and the *Massawomeck* as separate and discrete neighbors of the Powhatan's (Wright and Freund 1953: 57). However, this is the only instance in the primary sources where these synonyms occur in a context which makes them separate groups.

Royce (1881: 182) concluded that the several tribes which occupied the south shore of Lake Erie; the Massawomeckes, Erie, and Satanas or Chaouanons and the Shawnee; were one and the same people. He explains: "The Jesuits never succeeded in establishing contact with the Eries. Their intercourse with them was almost nothing and they left us no vocabularies by which their linguistic stock can be determined. I regard, therefore, the single volunteer remark as to their having the same language with the Hurons as having less weight in the scale of probabilities than the accumulated evidence of their identity with the Massawomeckes and Chaouanons."

Parkman (1899: 341) and Murray (1908: 44) speculate, without providing reasons, that the Massawomeck were Mohawk.

During the first quarter of this century several scholars published detailed papers which examined the tidewater Algonquians in the Chesapeake Bay region (Bushnell 1907; 1908; Mooney 1907; Speck 1907; 1924; Willoughby 1907). It is surprising that, apart from Bushnell's brief comment which notes that the Massawomeck made war on Powhatan (1907: 35), these otherwise definitive works do not mention the Massawomeck.

Hunt (1904: 23–24) accepted the Massawomeck on Chesapeake Bay in 1608 as a small band of marauders, but he noted that, "There is no

conclusive reason for supposing them to have been Iroquois." Referring
to Hunt's work, Fenton (1940: 235) supported this conclusion stating
" . . . there remains little likelihood that Smith's Massawomecke were
a party of Iroquois marauders." He suggests that they were more probably a war party from higher on the Susquehanna River. Schaeffer (1942:
vii) and Roy Wright (1974: 67) have supported Fenton's conclusion. Fenton hypothesizes (ibid.) that Champlain's *Carantouannais*, Brebeuf's *Scahentoarronons* "The People of the Big Flats," and Smith's *Massawomecke*
were components of a group which occupied the Susquehanna River
valley between the Susquehannock, below present day Harrisburg, and
the Mohawk to the north. He suggests these tribes were hostile to both
the Susquehannock and the Mohawk.

Hunt (1940: 186 n 2) argues that the Massawomeck who "do drive a
trade in Cannida" with the French prior to 1608, cannot be Erie because
Erie survivors did not meet the French until after their confederacy was
destroyed in 1656 and they were first seen by the French as captives in
Iroquois villages. Roy Wright (1974: 84–85) has challenged Hunt's thesis,
cogently pointing out that the dotted line on Champlain's map of 1632,
which is sometimes said to represent Brulé's route to the Carantouannais, may in fact mark an earlier French *coureur de bois* route into these
regions. Daillon's remarks (Thwaites, 1895–1901 (3): 809) regarding the
presence of the *coureur*   among the Neutral for some time prior to
1626 provides contemporary evidence to substantiate Wright's suggestion.

In his *Observations on Certain Ancient Tribes* Hoffman (1964) has examined in detail the relationship between the Massawomeck and a number of Iroquoians. Following his detailed examination of Swedish and
Dutch references in conjunction with the Lederer map of 1672 and the
Herrman map of 1673, Hoffman concluded: "The equivalence of the
names Massawomeck and Black Minqua [Erie] thus seems to be indicated strongly" (ibid.: 204). Weslager (1972:99) supports this identification. Hoffman also remarked that the "Evidence relating to the possible equivalence of the names Massawomeck and Erie is scanty, being
limited to the general correlation of the position indicated by the Smith
and Lederer maps with that indicated for the Erie (Eriehronon) by the
French sources" (ibid.: 204). Merrill (1979: 552, n 14) espouses the identification of the Massawomeck as Pocoughtranacks or Erie who were at
war with the Moyancer, the Piscataway.

On the basis of his examination of the early literature and the archaeological evidence, Hoffman (1964: 222) has concluded that the Massawomeck were either Whittlesey on the south shore of Lake Erie, or
Monongahela on the headwaters of the Monogahela and Youghiogheny
rivers in Pennsylvania.

Although not wholly germane in the context of this work, Hoffman's
investigation of Black Minqua and *Arrigahaga* connection with the Erie;

Black Minqua connections with the *Arrigahaga* and the *Richahecrian*; *Richahecrian* and *Rickohockan*[4] connections with the Erie; and *Richahecrian* connections with the *Rickohockan* provide the basis for a broader understanding of Indian groups in this region.

White (1978: 412) rejected Hoffman's (1964) proposal to extend Erie territory into Virginia " . . . by equating Erie, on the basis of similar cartographic locations, with the Pocaughtawonauck, Massawomeck, Massomack, Black Minqua, Arrigahaga, Richahecrian and Rickohockan." She concluded: "The assignment of such a vast area on the basis of weak and disputed evidence seems unacceptable and at odds with the size of territories identified with the Huron confederacy, the Iroquois league, or the Neutral" (ibid.).

More recently Menard and Carr (1982: 171, 186) have suggested that the Iroquois who raided the Piscataways on the Potomac River were the Seneca.

Swanton does not include the Massawomeck in his *Indian Tribes of North America* (1952) and they are mentioned but twice, both times only in passing, in the current *Handbook of North American Indians, Northeast*, Volume 15 (Trigger 1978).

---

[4] Hoffman's text regarding the *Rickohockans* does not include Smith's reference to the *Righkahauck* in his *True Relation* (Barbour 1969: 178), if indeed these are synonymous. *Righkahauck* was a Chickahominy village on the Chickahominy River which Smith visited in November or December 1607 (ibid.: 477). Mooney (1907: 131) identified the *Richahecrian* and the *Rickohockan* as Cherokee. On the other hand Swanton (1946: 111) has noted that, "It is now known quite definitely that the *Rechahecrians* (sic) who won the battle against the allied Powhatan Indians and the Virginia colonists in 1656 were not Cherokee, and there is no certainty that the *Rickohokans* of whom Lederer speaks were that tribe." Washburn (1978: 96) has raised the possibility that the *Rickohokans* were Iroquoians.

IV. DISCUSSION

There can be little doubt that some seventeenth century primary and contemporary accounts and maps are flawed. Smith's persistent location of the Massawomeck on a body of salt water in the hinterland, his European settlement at *Ocanahonan*, and the location of the *Atquanahucke* homeland in the interior are clear examples of misunderstood accounts related to him by the Indians. But Smith's misconceptions are not unique nor are others so readily reconcilable. Distortions undoubtedly attended the translation process in which Susquehannock Iroquoian accounts were translated into Tockwogh Algonquian before they were rendered to Smith in English or in a Powhatan dialect he could understand. However, attempts to detect and compensate for these distortions would likely create even greater errors. Apart from recognizing these "honest" mistakes, we need to be able to detect and understand the root causes for the deliberate exaggeration, or diminution, of events which were vital to the furtherance of the causes espoused by the principals, both Indian and European.

Fleet's *Journal* reflects the biases necessary to foster his trading interests in what appear to be his exaggerated estimates of the Massawomeck population and the quantities of beaver they had to trade, but there is no apparent self-serving reason why Fleet should be devious or misinformed regarding the identity of the *Hereckeene*, Erie, masquerading as Massawomeck or the four groups which he states comprised the Massawomeck "confederacy." Fleet's account of the number of days travel to the Massawomeck homeland may seek to conceal the location of his lucrative fur sources, but having been largely collaborated independently by Calvert's account two years later, this seems unlikely.

Champlain's accounts and his maps must also be regarded with reservation in this context. His information regarding the location of the *Antouhonorons* must have been derived from Indian accounts, but his comprehension of these relations, exemplified by his having first located the Neutral south of Lake Erie, does not inspire great confidence regarding his ability to place the *Antouhonorons*. Champlain too was the victim of misunderstanding, error, and translation distortions akin to those which plagued English accounts of events on Chesapeake Bay.

The cartographic evidence also merits notice in this regard. Although Smith differentiates between the regions depicted by his 1612 *Virginia* map which were recorded during his reconnaissances and those which he attributes to accounts by the Indians, this separation has been blurred, and French maps, which might appear to be independent

31

sources which confirm the location of the *Antouhonoron* territory in the Niagara region ca. 1616, are in fact derivative maps which simply repeat information provided earlier by Champlain.

With these general reservations in mind, we can examine the problems of Massawomeck identity, the location of their homeland, and several corollary matters.

IDENTITY

Edward Fleet's unique account of his eight-day stay with the Massomack (Massawomeck) in 1632 indicates they were a discrete group, possibly a tribe, governed by four 'kings'[1] whose towns, and possibly the "kings" too, were known as *Tonhoga* (Tohoga), *Mosticum* (Mostikum), *Shaunetowa*, and *Usserahak*. Significantly in this context the Usserahak and Mosticum Massawomeck made it clear to Fleet that they were not *Hereckeene*, (Neill 1876: 31; Wright 1974: 85), a synonym for the Erie, or a portion of that group. The information that Fleet planned to trade with all four of the Massawomeck "nations," each of which was governed by a "king" and *Usserahak* Massawomeck advice that the *Mosticums* were "one of their confederate nations," provides some idea of the Massawomeck political structure.[2] *Tonhoga, Mosticum, Shaunetowa,* and *Usserahak* were large settlements, the last allegedly having a population of 7,000. He also recounted visiting thirty Massawomeck palisaded villages, one of which had three hundred houses. By this account the Massawomeck population in 1632 far exceeded the five thousand Algonquians which Smith estimated to live within sixty miles of Jamestown ca. 1608.

The Massawomeck are conspicuous in English accounts of tidewater Chesapeake Bay Algonquians during the period 1607–1634, both as a result of the English having heard of their activities from the Indians and of Smith having encountered them once on the Bay. They appear on several seventeenth century English maps, none of which significantly enhances the documentary information available. Apart from the Delisle map of ca. 1700, the Massawomeck do not appear in French literature or on French maps at any time, by that name or any of the known synonyms. The inference is clear. Either the French did not know of the Pocoughtranack/Massawomeck/Massomack at all, or they knew them by a name which has not yet been equated with Massawomeck or any of its synonyms. Bearing in mind Susquehannock and Tockwogh

---

[1] Smith's *Virginia* map of 1612 indicates that in 1608 the Massawomeck had *three* "kings' houses." In 1632 Edward Fleet indicates there were *four* kings each with a village (Neill 1876: 27).

[2] McCary and Barka (1977: 64) suggest the "kings' houses" indicated on Smith's *Virginia* map were tribal capitals or political centers.

explanations to Smith in 1608 how the Massawomeck obtained European material from the French by that date, the latter option appears likely.

ACCESS TO CHESAPEAKE BAY

The route taken by the Massawomeck from their hinterland homeland to Chesapeake Bay during John Smith's era, ca. 1608, remains uncertain. Nevertheless, the record of their activities at tidewater generally is concentrated on the axis of the Potomac River. In 1607 shortly after the English arrived at Jamestown, Powhatan explained to Smith how the Massawomeck frequently attacked the Anacostank and Potomac in the region below the Great Falls of the Potomac (Arber 1884; cxiv; Barbour 1969: 186). Later from ca. 1627, events regarding the Massawomeck fur trade with the English recounted by Fleet are also centered on the Potomac River, as are the accounts of the Virginian and Marylander fur traders in 1632 and 1634. Significantly the Powell and Todkill relation also explains how on the lower reaches of the Potomac River from Point Lookout to the Wicomico River " . . . we could see no inhabitants" (Barbour 1969: 402). This is the region, which by 1634, the Yaocomicos were forced to abandon to avoid being harassed by raiding Susquehannock. Possibly the Susquehannock raids along the west shore date from ca. 1608, although that is not collaborated by Smith's account that they knew little of Powhatan and he as little of them (Quinn 1979 (5): 323).

The Massawomeck may also have entered Chesapeake Bay on one of the rivers which flow into the Bay between the Patuxent and Susquehanna rivers. Russell and Todkill related how in that region for " . . . 30 leagues we sailed more Northwards not finding any inhabitants yet the coast [be] well watered" (Barbour 1969: 402; Quinn 1979 (5): 320). Later they noted again that "thirty leagues Northward [from the Patuxent River] is a river not inhabited, yet navigable, for the red earth or clay resembling bole Armoniak the English calld it *Bolus*" (Barbour 1969: 342). It was off this *Bolus* river, the present-day Patapsco River, that Smith met the Massawomeck party crossing the Bay in canoes in 1608 (Barbour 1969: 406; Quinn 1979 (5): 322). At the head of Chesapeake Bay at an uncertain location where it divides in two channels and farther on into four, Smith found these channels uninhabited (ibid.). The information contained in the instructions Gates received in 1608, while erroneous in part, recounts how the Massawomeck make " . . . continual incursions upon . . . all those that inhabit the Rivers of the Bolus . . . " (Barbour 1969: 267). Jefferson (Bozman 1837: 112–14; Peden 1955) has suggested that the Massawomeck came to the coastal regions through " . . . the back parts of Pennsylvania and entered Chesapeake Bay at the Bush River . . . " immediately south of the mouth of the Susquehanna River.

It does not seem likely that the Massawomeck gained entry to Chesapeake Bay on the Susquehanna River although it has been suggested that they " . . . paddled their bark canoes down the Susquehanna" to tidewater (Weslager 1983: 27, 33).[3] Massawomeck-Susquehannock hostility, which has been stressed in the primary and contemporary records, does not suggest that the Susquehanna River would be open to the Massawomeck within the territory dominated by the Susquehannock.

In concert these accounts suggest that there was an unpopulated corridor from the Bay to the hinterland, a no-man's-land, between the Patuxent and Susquehanna rivers through which the Massawomeck traveled to Chesapeake Bay ca. 1608, having left the Potomac River at some point above Great Falls. Whether this region was uninhabited because it was the route followed by the greatly feared Massawomeck, or an uninhabited region used by the Massawomeck to avoid the populated Potomac River axis below Great Falls, is uncertain. Probably both were factors in the selection of a secure Massawomeck route to and from the Bay.

TRADE

Gallatin (1836) has suggested that the Massawomeck party encountered by Smith on Chesapeake Bay in 1608 were " . . . probably Iroquois fulfilling their career of conquest." Fenton (1940: 235) believed them to be a war party whose homeland was on the Susquehanna River above the Susquehannock homeland. Certainly Powhatan's relation in 1607 and subsequent English accounts of Massawomeck attacks at the head of the Bay and on the Piscataway and the Potomac on the axis of the Potomac River (Barbour 1969: 186) indicate that Massawomeck intrusions into these regions were hostile.

This hostility on the west shore of the Bay and at the head of the Bay stands in sharp contrast to Smith's remarks regarding Massawomeck relations with the bands he visited on the east side of the Bay south of Tangier Sound (Hewitt 1907 (1): 7) in the summer of 1608. There the *Kuskarawocke, Soraphanigh, Nause, Arsek* and *Natuaquake*[4] " . . . much ex-

---

[3] A cartouche in the lower left corner of the Augustin Herrman map of 1673 states in part that the Susquehanna River is: ". . . full of falls and isles until about 10 or 12 miles above the Sasquahana fort [Canooge in the Lancaster Pa. area] then it runs clear but Downwards not navigable but with greater danger with Indian Canooe by Indian Pilots."

[4] Strachey (Wright and Freund 1953: 57) states that Powhatan had dominion over ". . . some petty Nations on the East syde of our bay." These bands include the *Accohanock* and *Accomack* which lie to the south of the Nanticoke bands on Tangier Sound. Both Smith (Barbour 1969: 344) and Strachey (Wright and Freund 1953: 57) indicate these bands were under Powhatan's suzerainty. Subsequently scholars have supported this affiliation (Brinton 1884: 226; Hodge 1907 (1): 7; Barbour 1969: 169, 1986 (2): 107). Speck (1928: 233, 287), following Mooney's (1907) lead, places the *Accohanoc*, the *Accomac*, and other Algonquian bands south of the modern Maryland line under Powhatan suzerainty while those to the north of that line were practically independent. However, he goes on to suggest that because these bands spoke the Powhatan dialect they can be considered to be in Powhatan's confederacy. While that arrangement may have served Speck's purpose to cluster these bands linguistically, this work will emphasize Smith's explanation that at least some of these bands "extolled" Powhatan's enemy the Massawomeck, an option not enjoyed by Powhatan's bands on the west shore of the Bay and only after ca. 1627 by the Conoy bands to the north.

tolled a great nation called Massawomecks" (Barbour 1969: 401; Quinn 1979 (5): 320). Tooker (1894: 181) has suggested that in this context "much extolled" indicates these bands were friendly with, and in some manner allied to, the Massawomeck who came to this region to trade furs for marine shell beads, " . . . as the work *Kuskarwoke* denotes." Having had an opportunity to reflect upon his Jamestown experiences, Smith concluded in 1624 in his *General Historie* (1624: 61) that he had found the bands in the Tangier Sound region who traded with the Massawomeck were " . . . the best merchants of all other savages." Significantly, when Powhatan recounted to Smith the names of his bands who were preyed upon by the Massawomeck, he made no mention of these eastern shore bands having been attacked. Barbour's map (1969: 169), which purports to indicate the extent of Powhatan's suzerainty, also excludes the bands on the Tangier Sound from his dominions.

There is good evidence to indicate that Massawomeck intrusions into these regions would be advantageous. By 1608 a significant quantity of European material was concentrated in this region. As Smith explained: " . . . now by trucking [trading] they have plenty of the forme [tool types] of yron. An these are their Chief instruments and arms" (Barbour 1969: 358). Strachey confirms this assessment of plenty remarking how " . . . by trucking with us they have thousands of our iron hatchets such as they are" (Wright and Freund 1953: 107).

These Massawomeck raiding and trading activities in the Chesapeake Bay region where European material was readily available by 1608 resulted in the movement westward of both European goods and marine shells, particularly *Busycon laeostomum*, generally on the axis of the Potomac River to the Massawomeck homelands and beyond to the Neutral, Petun and Huron (Pendergast 1989). But this concentration of European material in the hands of Chesapeake Bay Indians cannot be attributed to the Jamestown colonists alone. In May 1607 soon after the colonists arrived and before the presence of the settlers had significantly increased the quantity of European goods available in this region, a delegation from Jamestown, which included George Percy, visited the *Apamatick* (Appamatuck), their Algonquian neighbors nearby on the James River. There Percy remarked upon seeing " . . . pieces of yron able to cleave a man in sunder" (Barbour 1969: 138).

The concentration of European material in this region long predated the establishment of the Jamestown colony in 1607. In addition to the

---

Strachey's hearsay advice (Wright and Freund 1953: 56) that the Tockwoghs were under Powhatan's dominion is discounted somewhat by his earlier information (ibid.: 49) that they, like the *Kuskarawoaks*, were in the "envyron" of Powhatan's empire. Certainly Smith's account of Tockwogh relations with the Susquehannock in 1608 does not suggest that they were under Powhatan suzerainty. This is borne out by Smith's statement in his 1612 *Map of Virginia* which states that the people at the head of the Bay, which includes Tockwogh, ". . . are scarce known to Powhatan" (Barbour 1969: 343) and by the Powell and Todkill account in *The Proceedings* which states that ". . . these know no more of the territories of Powhatan then [sic] his names and he as little of them" (Barbour 1969: 408; Quinn 1979 (5): 323). Smith repeats the Powell and Todkill account in his *General Historie* (1624: 61).

English colonization attempt at Roanoke over the period 1584–1606, numerous Spanish, French, and English voyages are known to have entered the Bay prior to 1607.[5] These, together with numerous unrecorded European visits which can neither be demonstrated nor denied, provided ample opportunity for significant quantities of European goods to have been acquired by the Indians in these latitudes before the arrival of the Jamestown colonists. Contemporary records do not indicate that there was a comparable concentration of European material elsewhere south of Norumbega, generally south of Cape Cod, prior to 1600, which would serve to attract marauding hinterland Iroquoians in search of European goods in the sixteenth century.[6]

This image of plenty in the Chesapeake Bay region may appear to be at variance with isolated English accounts if they are taken out of context. For instance, Edward Wingfield's contemporary account describes how in 1608 an Indian messenger from Powhatan to the English at Jamestown

---

[5] The *recorded* voyages to the Chesapeake Bay latitudes prior to 1607 include the Verrazano landing on the Delmarva Peninsula in 1524 where he kidnapped an Indian boy; the possibility of Quexos having been in Chesapeake Bay in 1525; the Spanish voyages which resulted in the Bay being recorded first on the world map of Juan Vespucci of 1526 and the description of the Bay set out in Alonso de Chaves's unpublished *Quatripartitum Opus* of 1536 or 1537 (Cumming 1982: 275, 277); Velasco's account of English seamen having been in the Chesapeake Bay several times before 1546; the presence of a French privateer trading in the Bay in 1546; the presence of the Vilafañe supply ship at Axacan inside the Bay in 1561 when Don Luis was kidnapped; the massacre and plunder of the Jesuit Axacan mission in 1570; the Menéndez de Avilés punitive expedition to Axacan in 1572; voyages associated with the founding of the Roanoke settlement in 1585; Lane's exploration to the foot of Chesapeake Bay over the winter 1585-1586; the English ship taking on fresh water in Chesapeake Bay in 1586; the introduction of additional settlers at Roanoke by White in 1587; the English ship that took on water in Chesapeake Bay in 1587; the extensive reconnaissance of Chesapeake Bay to the mouth of the Susquehanna River by González in 1588 and the secret voyages commissioned by Ralegh to rescue the Roanoke settlers after 1586, even as late as 1608 (Quinn 1979).

Unrecorded voyages, some of which undoubtedly also introduced European material into Chesapeake Bay, are indicated by the English and French privateers and pirates who frequented this coast. Some of these, as is evidenced by the French ship in 1546, entered and traded in Chesapeake Bay (Quinn 1979 (1): 217). Probably Portuguese fishermen also entered the Bay. Since the first decade of the sixteenth century they had annually sailed northward to the fishing banks of Baccalaos (Quinn 1979 (1): 278).

[6] As late as 1605 Champlain specifically noted how in Norumbega the Armouchiquois were still dependent upon stone tools, except for a few metal axes they had obtained from Acadia (Biggar 1921: 338). In 1609 on Lake Champlain when Champlain first met the Iroquois, probably the Mohawk, he noted their use of stone tools and a few ". . . poor [metal] axes which they sometimes win in a war. . . " (Biggar 1925: 96). At present the orthodoxy suggests that this European material originated in the Newfoundland-Gulf of St. Lawrence latitudes to the exclusion of all other regions. Unless convincing *evidence* can demonstrate the exclusivity of the St. Lawrence region in this regard, longstanding documentation which demonstrates the presence of Europeans in Chesapeake Bay and Norumbega (Feest 1978, 1978 (a), 1978 (b); Quinn 1977, 1979) (5) cannot be overlooked as credible evidence of an equally plausible source for the material seen by Champlain in 1609. It should be noted in this connection that there is no *record* of Europeans being on the Hudson River, or on the Atlantic coast in that region, before the Dutch ca. 1609, apart from Verrazano in 1524. This explanation is not intended to deny that by 1580, possibly by 1562, the St. Lawrence region was a growing source for European material (Le Blant et Beaudry 1967; Pendergast 1985).

was rewarded by the English " . . . with many trifles which were great wonders to him" (Quinn 1979 (5): 277). First-hand accounts by Smith (Quinn 1979 (5): 322), Percy (Barbour 1969: 138), and Strachey (Wright and Freund 1953: 75, 101) regarding the presence, indeed the abundance, of European material present in the tidewater regions by 1607, suggest that perhaps it was the exotic nature of the particular trifles this messenger received that caused him great wonder. Had he been given a European item then commonly encountered in that region, possibly an iron hatchet, he might not have reacted in a manner likely to cause Wingfield to comment.

At present no great antiquity can be attributed to the Massawomeck practice of seeking European material at tidewater; it appears to have become commonplace within Powhatan's lifetime. Nevertheless, accounts by Powhatan in 1607 indicate that the *Moyoancer* (Piscataway) had long been harassed by the Massawomeck (Barbour 1969: 186), and remarks by the Jamestown settlers indicating that the Susquehannock and Tockwogh were " . . . continually tormented by them" (ibid.: 361, 401; Weslager 1983: 32), and Strachey's explanation that " . . . the *Pattawomecks* the *Pawtuxunts* the *Susquesahanoughs* the *Tockwoghs* are contynually harrowed and frightened by them" (Wright and Freund 1953: 107) indicate that marauding Massawomecks had been present at tidewater for some time prior to 1607. The Susquehannock and Tockwogh experiences related to Smith in 1608 at the head of Chesapeake Bay also suggests that marauding in this region also enjoyed some antiquity.

The Massawomeck attack on the Tockwogh village and their willingness to be coaxed aboard Smith's boat in July 1608 provides some idea of Massawomeck determination to acquire European goods even in the face of danger. Their readiness to trade even their weapons to Smith in return for European trifles while still deep in enemy territory reveals the extent to which they were prepared to go and the extent to which the Massawomeck dominated the region and the contempt in which they held these Algonquian bands. Even while deep in Algonquian territory, a few Massawomeck had no particular fear of being attacked by the tidewater Algonquians said to be some 5,000 strong at that time. Smith's encounter with the Massawomeck canoe party is reminiscent of Jacques Cartier's experience on the Bay of Chaleur in 1534. There too the Indians, in this case Micmac, demonstrated their eagerness to trade with Europeans. Whether these Micmac and Massawomeck had had previous but unrecorded trading experience with Europeans remains to be demonstrated, but certainly both reacted quickly to exploit the opportunity at hand to obtain European goods.

Smith's encounter with the Patawomeck (Potomac) in June 1608, during his return voyage southward along the west shore of Chesapeake Bay following his visit to the Tockwogh village, is noteworthy. Although the *Potomac* and probably their neighbors the *Moyaones* (Piscataway), *Nacothtant* (Anacostank), and *Taux* (Patuxent); had been " . . . commanded to betray us by Powhatan's direction," they "kindly used" Smith and his party (Barbour 1969: 403). This does not suggest that these bands on the northern environs of Powhatan's dominions were, at this time, wholly subordinate to Powhatan, as sometimes has been suggested (McCary 1957: 6). Indeed, this loose affiliation of Algonquian bands on the periphery of Powhatan's "empire" on the west shore of the Bay indicates how by 1608 the Nanticoke bands on the east shore of the Bay south of Tangier Sound were able to establish and maintain an amicable trading relationship with the Massawomeck while the core of Powhatan's Algonquian "empire" remained hostile to them.

The trading patterns which were extant in Chesapeake Bay ca. 1608 were not immutable. By 1627 there is no evidence that the Massawomeck were trading with the Nanticoke bands on the east side of the Bay in the Tangier Sound region. Nor is there any record of their having attacked the Susquehannock and Tockwogh at the head of the Bay, although these raids may have continued unrecorded. By that date they have developed a more secure source of European goods adjacent to their new homeland in the Chesapeake Bay hinterland. Following a punitive campaign against the Moyancer Piscataway ca. 1627 in which large numbers of Piscataway were killed (Neill 1876: 25; Menard and Carr 1982: 186), the Massawomeck established suzerainty over the Potomac River Conoy bands, forcing them to acquiesce to arrangements whereby the Anacostank, and to a lesser extent the Piscataway, served as middlemen in the Massawomeck fur trade with the Virginians and Marylanders (Neill 1876; Hoffman 1967: 8, 38 n. 3; Feest 1978 a: 243). Undoubtedly these Conoy bands sought to dilute Massawomeck control when they met with Calvert and Fleet in 1634 to negotiate an association with the English (Menard and Carr 1982: 171). Possibly they were successful, for this is the last year the Massawomeck are known to have been trading on Chesapeake Bay.

THE FRENCH CONNECTION

Powhatan's relation to Smith in 1607 is the earliest English evidence of a connection between New France on the St. Lawrence River and the Chesapeake Bay region. At that time Powhatan indicated to Smith how at *Ocanahonan*, an unknown location beyond the headwaters of the James River and on a sea beyond the "Quirank" mountains, there lived people who wore European clothing and sailed in European ships. *Ocanahonan* was said to be located on the "same sea" as the Pocoughtronack (Massawomeck) (Barbour 1969:182–83, 186). This explanation has raised the possibility that the identification of *Ocanahonan* could help locate the Massawomeck homeland. The possibility has also arisen that the Europeans at *Ocanahonan* may have been the source of the French European goods the Massawomeck are alleged to have obtained on the "river of

Cannida," as the Susquehannock and Tockwogh related to Smith in 1608. However, an examination of the evidence concerning *Ocanahonan* (Appendix 'B') demonstrates conclusively that there is no connection between *Ocanahonan* and the Massawomeck. Again, Smith had misunderstood the briefing he had received from Powhatan in 1607.

Probably the best-known account of a Massawomeck connection with the French on the St. Lawrence River is set out by Nathaniel Po(w)ell and Anas Todkill in the *Proceedings*. In this work they recount how during Smith's meeting with the Susquehannock in a Tockwogh Algonquian village they heard in July 1608: " . . . many description and discourses they made us of Atquanahucke, Massawomeck and other people, signifying they inhabit the river of Cannida, and from the French to have their hatchets, and such tools by trade . . . " (Barbour 1969: 408; Quinn 1979 (5): 323).

This text requires close scrutiny to discern that the Susquehannock are explaining to Smith that it is the Massawomeck who obtain European material from the French. Later when Powhatan corrected Smith regarding the location of the Atquanahucke homeland making it clear that they lived on Delaware Bay, he removed the Atquanahucke from those who lived on the "river of Cannida" and those who received European material from the French in New France (Smith 1624: 61). Remarkably it has long been contended that it was the Susquehannock who were trading with the French to the north and so served as middlemen to redistribute this French material from the north and at the head of Chesapeake Bay (Stith 1747: 69; Hunter 1959: 13; Quinn 1977: 451; Ceci 1977: 71; Brasser 1978: 81; Feest 1978 (a): 255; Cumming 1982: 281; Jennings 1982: 219; Trigger 1985: 143, 155; 1988: 257–8). David Quinn (1973: 459) has suggested that the heavy iron weapons "able to cleave a man in sunder" seen by George Percy in the Appamatuck village on the James River in 1607 (Purchas 1625(18): 412; Barbour 1969: 138) may have been obtained "through" the Iroquois traveling to the St. Lawrence River to trade with the French.

Francis Magnel's *Relation of the First Voyage at the Beginning of the Jamestown* (1610) states in part: " . . . the natives of Virginia assure them [the English] that on the other side of Virginia by the South Sea there is a land where the natives wear long silk robes and buskins, and that they have a great deal of gold, and that ships often come to the said land which bargain with the natives there and take gold and silk from there, and in proof of this those of Virginia showed the English some knives and other things which they got from those who came in the said ships, and the English judge that the said ships would be Spanish" (Barbour 1969: 156). Nevertheless, there is at present, no evidence to demonstrate the reality of the Tockwogh and Susquehannock accounts which claimed that, commencing before 1608, the Massawomeck had obtained " . . . hatchets and such tooles by trade" from the French on a regular basis. There are, however, accounts of events in 1634 by several independent sources which support the credibility of a trading connection between the Canada region on the St. Lawrence River and the hinterland Massawomeck and *Hereckeenes* Erie who lived between Chesapeake Bay and lakes Ontario and Erie. Principal among these is Fleet's account which relates how in July 1632 while trading with the *Hereckeenes* Erie he saw in their possession two English axes. By Fleet's account these axes were the type Sir David Kirke traded at Quebec during the period 1629–1632. It is interesting to note that he (Fleet) identified these axes as being identical to the axes he had obtained from "Whitts of Wapping" in London for his use in the English fur trade on Chesapeake Bay. The *Hereckeenes* could have been regaling Fleet with tales of trade with the English in the Canada region to obtain some trading advantage by perfidiously displaying English axes which in fact they had acquired on Chesapeake Bay, but this seems unlikely in the light of subsequent events.

Soon after Fleet had seen the English axes with the *Hereckeenes*, the *Massawomeck* fur traders of Great Falls related to Smith the reputation of the *Hereckeenes* as the "Cannyda Indians" who did " . . . drive a trade in Canada at a plantation which is fifteen days journey from this place," their homeland. In May 1634 Calvert confirmed these accounts of the trading connections with the Canada region by relating how the English colonists on Chesapeake Bay had lost access to some 3000 beaver pelts when their trading partners, the Massawomeckes, had recently directed all their trade to Kirke at Quebec. Certainly there was a concentration of European material on the St. Lawrence River by this date. French traders had ascended the St. Lawrence River as far as the Lachine Rapids by 1580, possibly as early as 1562 (Le Blant et Beaudry 1967; Pendergast 1985), but the Hereckeenes and Massawomeck may not have had to travel to the St. Lawrence River to obtain European goods. Daillon's letter (Sagard 1636) indicates how prior to 1626 French *coureurs de bois* had visited *Ouontisation*, a Neutral village at the head of Lake Ontario one day's journey from the Seneca: "Many of our Frenchmen who have been here [at *Ounontisaston*] have in the past made journeys to this country and to the Neutral Nation for the sake of reaping profit and advantage from the furs."[7] Roy Wright (1974: 85) has suggested that the dotted line south of a much distorted Lake Erie on Champlain's map of 1632, which is sometimes said to be Brulé's route to the Carantouannais in 1615, may in fact represent an early coureur de bois trading route into those regions which was in use by that date.

This evidence of the Hereckeene Erie having traded with the French before ca. 1632 contrasts sharply with current orthodoxy which holds that the French did not encounter the Erie until after 1656 when they

---

[7] A considerably less detailed account of Daillon's experiences at *Ouontisaston* appears in the *Jesuit Relation* for 1640-41 (Thwaites 1895-1901 (21): 203-205).

were first seen as captives among the Five Nation Iroquois. However, because the evidence in support of the Hereckeene Erie having traded in the Canada region relates to a period prior to 1634, and 1632 in particular, it may be that it took place over the period 1629–1632 when the English under Kirke occupied Quebec. In that event the French may not have encountered the Hereckeene Erie in this context.

There is additional evidence that hinterland Iroquians could have obtained European goods introduced by the English on the axis of the St. Lawrence River without their having to go to Quebec. Soon after the Kirke brothers occupied Quebec in July 1629 there arose a conflict between the Kirkes and a group represented by Sir William Alexander. Matters were resolved when the two factions joined to form the *Company of Adventurers to Canada*. Moir records (1966: 405) that this Company " . . . prosecuted the fur trade, contended with attempts to trade by both French and English interlopers, maintained two hundred men in Canada, and explored 400 leagues into the interior." This suggests there was ample opportunity for frontier and hinterland tribes to acquire European goods introduced by the English during the Kirke interlude without their traveling to the Canada region on the St. Lawrence River. It also enhances the credibility of the Massawomeck explanation that the Hereckeenes traded for European material at a "plantation" fifteen days journey from their homeland. Heretofore there has been little to support the possibility of European traders, particularly English ones, in the Iroquoian hinterland. This too explains, in part, the two English axes from Whitts of Wapping, London, which Fleet saw with the Hereckeenes on the Potomac in 1532 and Calvert's explanation that the Marylanders had arrived too late in 1534 to have access to the furs which were traded to the Kirkes at Quebec.

LINGUISTICS

In his 1612 *Map of Virginia* John Smith remarked upon the variety of languages which were spoken in the regions surrounding Chesapeake Bay. In particular he noted: " . . . many several nations of sundry languages that environ Powhatan's Territories. The *Chowanokes* [Algonquians], the *Mangoags* [southern Iroquians], the *Manacans*, and *Mannahokes* [both are eastern Siouans], the *Massawomeckes* [northern Iroquoians], the *Powhatan* [Algonquians], the *Susquesahanocks* [northern Iroquoians], the *Atquanachukes*, [Algonquians], the *Tockwoghes* [Nanticoke Algonqian]. Al those not any one understandeth another but by Interpreters" (Barbour 1969: 344; 1986 (2): 107; Smith 1624: 25; Wright and Freund 1953: 49). Accounts of Smith's encounter with the Massawomeck crossing Chesapeake Bay in canoes indicate clearly that, except by signs, he was wholly unable to communicate with them (Barbour 1969: 407). Neither could the Massawomeck converse in any of the Algonquian dialects in which Smith had demonstrated a competence nor in the dialects used by his interpreters to communicate with the various Algonquian bands Smith encountered on his journey around the Bay.

Several scholars have sought to identify the Massawomeck linguistic affiliation. In 1881 Gatschet interpreted "Massawomecke" to be Algonquian for *those on a great water* which, he suggests, is in keeping with the lacustrine homeland location attributed to them by the Susquehannock and the Tockwogh. Having examined Edward Fleet's 1632 record of the Massawomeck words for town and band names in conjunction with words which Margry indicates were recorded by La Salle in the Lake Erie region in 1699, and in conjunction with the words recorded by Abbé de Gallinée (Réné de Brehant de Gallinée) who accompanied La Salle, Gatschet concluded:

From all facts stated it becomes apparent that the "Herechenes" were not included in the term *Massawomecke*, but that this term comprehended at least one of the Five Nations, The *Senecas*, and that the three others [mentioned by Fleet] were allied or confederated with them. Indian history sufficiently proves that it is more natural to suppose racial and linguistic affinity between the four chieftaincies of the Massawomeckes [Fleet gives four, Smith indicates three], than to build them up of tribes of disparate affinities and heterogeneous elements. What we cannot possibly decide now, for want of sufficient information, is whether the three other tribes formed, with the *Shaunetowa*, the four villages of the Senecas mentioned by Gallinée, or whether they were scattered all the way from Lake Ontario to the Ohio River, as the name *Tonhoga* seems to indicate. To assume that the Massawomeckes were the Shawnees would be to assume they had formed an alliance with the *Shaunetowa*, or Seneca" (Gatschet 1881: 322–24).

Tooker (1894: 183) argues Massawomecke is an Algonquian word meaning *those who go and come by boat*, or *those who travel by boat*.

Hewitt (1910: 658–59) concluded that of the twelve populous sedentary tribes listed in the *Jesuit Relation* for 1635 (Thwaites 1895–1901 (8): 115) as dwelling south of the French settlements, the *Scahentoarronons*, or *Akhrakvaerton* as they were known in Huron, were *probably* the Massawomeck. He derived this identification from a linguistic analysis of a number of Iroquoian and Algonquian roots. Hewitt translated *Scahentowanenrhonons* as *people beyond big meadows*. This was the Huron and Iroquois word for the Wyoming plain on the Susquehanna River in the vicinity of present day Wilkes-Barre. Hewitt (1910: 658) quotes Heckewelder's suggestion that *Wyoming* is a Delaware cognate term derived from a translation of the Iroquois word. Heckewelder indicated *M'cheuómi* or *M'cheuwámi* signifies "extensive level flats" in Delaware. The Delaware locative term would be *M'cheóming* or *M'cheuwáming* meaning "at the great flats or plains" which the English changed into Wyoming. The animate plural added to the first of these locative terms would produce

M'cheuomek which, Hewitt contends, Smith heard in another Algonquian dialect as *Massawomecke*.

Two entries in the Jesuit *Journal* for 1652 indicate the Iroquois defeated the *Atra'kwae'ronnons* or *Adasto'e'ronnons* that year. Hewitt suggests that the identification of the *Atra'kwa'e* as *Andasto'e* " . . . is probably due to a misconception of the relator." He supported this identification of the Massawomeck by drawing attention to the fact that Smith, on his 1612 map *Virginia* and Champlain on his 1632 map indicate that the Massawomeck and the Carantouannais respectively both have three "King houses" or towns. Interpreting Smith's observations somewhat subjectively when he introduces the Potomac River specifically, Hewitt noted that the Massawomeck were located "beyond the mountains from whence is the head of the river Potawomeck . . . " and " . . . higher up in the mountains . . . " than the Susquehannock. He concluded, "These references to the presence of mountains in the country of the Massawomeckes well describe the mountainous regions of the upper Susquehanna r[iver] and its branches," including the Wyoming Flats area.

Fenton (1940: 232–39) has suggested there were at least two groups of Iroquoians on the Susquehanna River. Those on the lower reaches of the river were the *roily water people*, known to the French and Huron as the Andaste, or Andastoerrhonon or Ganadstoguehronons and to the English as the Susquehannock or Conestoga and as the *Minqua* or *White Minqua* to the Dutch and Swedes. By Smith's account they were located some fifty miles above the rocks near present day Port Deposit, Maryland, which marked the head of navigation, or possibly at Falmouth Falls south of Canewago Creek (Hewitt 1910: 654; Fenton 1940: 237). Fenton's second group were the *big flats people* or the *Skahendawaneh-ronon*, Hewitt's *Scahentowanenrhonons*, and Brébeuf's *Scahentoarrhonons* (Thwaites 1895–1901 (8): 115), who were on the North Branch of the Susquehanna River on the Wyoming Flats above present day Wilkes-Barre. Fenton suggests they were also Smith's *Massawomeck* and Brule's *Carantouannais* (Biggar 1929: 217, 1632 map).

In support of this conclusion Fenton examined the location of the six Susquehannock villages shown on Smith's 1612 *Virginia* map and the location of the tribes shown on the Dutch *Carte Figurative* of ca. 1614 drawn by the Dutch fur trader Adriaen Blockx (Cummings et al 1971; 265) and redrawn by William Blaeu for his *Novus Atlas* (Goss 1990a:164; 1990b:68). As a result he presented the following three-faceted argument used by Hewitt to equate the Massawomecke and Wyoming, quoting as references Hewitt's correspondence with Stirling dated 20 December 1936, and Bureau of American Ethnology Ms. No. 3816:

1. "The linguistic equivalence of Algonquian Massawomecke and Wyoming to Iroquoian Scahentoa—and Carantouan [Skahentawaneh]—meaning "big grassy flat";
2. "The similar position and number of towns of the Massawomecke,

have three kings' houses on Smith's map of Virginia, 1612, and the Carantouannais, whom Brulé assigned three towns"; and

3. "Brébeuf's enumeration of the Iroquois tribes in 1635 (Thwaites Jesuit Relations, vol. 8, p. 115) . . . Andastoerrhonons (Susquehanna), Scahentoarrhonons (Wyoming), Riierhonons (Erie), and Ahouenrochrhons (Wenro), which clearly shows his Huron informants considered them distinct tribes."

Current archaeological data do not support Fenton's hypothesis. The McFate-Quiggle sites on the West Branch of the Susquehanna River and the archaeological sites in the Wyoming Valley which, having yielded no European material, are attributed to a prehistoric period prior to the arrival of Europeans. Both these peoples are believed to have been destroyed ca. 1525–1550, by the Susquehannock Iroquoians when the latter moved southward from Bradford County at the junction of the Chemung and Susquehanna rivers to Lancaster County near Chesapeake Bay, where their archaeological sites date from ca. 1600. After the inhabitants of the Wyoming Valley were destroyed by the Susquehannocks that region remained uninhabited until the Algonquian Conoy bands and Nanticoke moved into that region ca. 1730.[8]

Michael Foster (pers. comm. 1987) having examined the Massawomeck words for their kings and villages (*To(n)hoga, Usserahak, Shaunnetowa,* and *Mosticum*) has opined that apart from *Mosticum* they are "possible—even likely—Iroquoian words." *To(n)hoga* is a plausible Iroquoian word which could mean something like "the junction of two creeks or small rivers (Lounsbury 1960: 53), although there is too much distortion to be certain. *Usserahak* is more certainly an Iroquoian word." Foster explains it consists of a noun root meaning "basswood." Fenton (per. comm. 1987) has suggested "basswood opening." Chafe (1967: 55, item 646) indicates that the modern Seneca name for present day Buffalo, New York, is "basswood." This connection, however tenuous, ac-

---

[8] During the fifteenth and the first half of the sixteenth centuries, several groups occupied the Susquehanna River valley. The McFate-Quiggle people were located on the West Branch, the Wyoming Valley people were in the vicinity of Wilkes-Barre, and the Shenks Ferry people were in Lancaster County, Pennsylvania near the Maryland line. Initially and prior to ca. 1550 the Susquehannock were located in Bradford County, Pennsylvania, near the junction of the Susquehanna and Chemung rivers near the New York state line. Circa 1550 the Susquehannock left their homeland in Bradford County in the north to move southward through the Susquehanna River valley to the region south of present day Lancaster, Pennsylvania, near the mouth of the Susquehanna River.

The archaeological material excavated on McFate-Quiggle sites on the West Branch and that on Wyoming Valley Complex sites in the vicinity of Wilkes-Barre indicate that these people were not Susquehannocks. Nor is there any evidence of European material on these sites. Having no evidence that they moved elsewhere intact, they are believed to have been destroyed *in-situ* during the period 1525-1550 by the Susquehannock when they moved southward through these regions to the new Susquehannock homeland in Lancaster County. One thing is certain. By the time the Susquehannock had moved through and beyond the West Branch and Wilkes-Barre regions, these areas were no longer in-

cords well with the initial location of the Massawomeck in the Niagara Frontier region ca. 1608 as postulated here.[9]

Foster goes on: "*Shaunetowa* is plausibly Iroquoian and the final element *owa* strongly suggests one form of an Iroquoian root meaning large, great, or grand. While there is a superficial resemblance to the early French name for the Seneca, too much distortion would be necessary to make that a serious connection." Foster also raises the possibility "whether *Shaunetowa* could be a form of an Iroquoian word which has come down to us both as *Skenondoah* and *Skenandore*, the Susquehanna River and an Oneida family name *Skennontonah* or *Skennontonha*" (Lounsbury 1960: 65). In that event the meaning could be "deer," an important Iroquoian moiety or clan, particularly in the Huron. In this context it is interesting to compare these Massawomeck names with the Susquehannock clans and nations as they were recorded in 1666: *Dahadaghesa*, the Turtle clan; *Sarangararo*, the Wolf clan; *Gosweinquecrakqua*, the Fox clan; *Waskanecqua* of the *Ohongeoquena* nation; *Kagoregago* of the *Unquehiett* nation; *Saraqundett* of the *Kaiquariegahaga* nation; *Uwhanhierelera* of the *Usququhaga* nation and *Waddonhago* of the *Sconondihago* nation (Hewitt 1910: 653–54). A Deer clan is not included.

---

habited and continued to be uninhabited until ca. 1730 when Conoy Algonquian bands and Nanticoke moved into the region in colonial times.

In Bradford County, the prehistoric home of the Susquehannock, the protohistoric Susquehannock archaeological sites contain a small amount of European material, usually scraps of metal (Dunbar and Ruhl 1974). These sites are dated ca. 1550, slightly later than the McFate-Quiggle sites on the West Branch and the Wyoming Valley Complex in the Wilkes-Barre area where no European goods attributable to this era have been excavated.

Upon their arrival in Lancaster County near the mouth of Susquehanna River ca. 1575 the Susquehannock encountered the indigenous Shenks Ferry people. Conflict and European disease soon depleted the Shenks Ferry people so that over the period 1575-1600 their survivors were assimilated by the Susquehannock. From this time onward, through to the period when the Susquehannock encountered Smith in 1608, the Susquehannock occupied what is now Lancaster County. Archaeological sites in this region which have been attributed to this period; the Washington Boro site ca. 1600-1625, the Roberts and Billmeyer sites ca. 1625-1645 and the Strickler site ca. 1645-1665 and later sites all contain large amounts of European material which, with the possible exception of certain glass beads, cannot be demonstrated to have been introduced by a specific European national group, or attributed to a particular documented encounter between natives and Europeans.

This understanding of Susquehanna River Valley archaeology does not support a hypothesis in which ca. 1600 the Susquehannock located at the head of Chesapeake Bay served as middlemen to distribute European material they received from a northern source. While it accords well with the hypothesis which ca. 1635 has the "roily water people" living along the lower river at the falls (Fenton 1940: 232), there is no archaeological evidence to support a second group, "the big flats people," on the North Branch above Wyoming (ibid.). Archaeological evidence indicates that the Wyoming area near Wilkes-Barre was uninhabited from ca. 1525 when the Wyoming Valley Complex was destroyed until ca. 1730 when Conoy Nanticoke established a village, the Knouse site, in this area (Kent 1984: 18, 122-23, 306-307, 401).

(This synopsis of Susquehanna River valley archaeology is derived from several sources, principally Witthoft 1969, Kinsey 1969, Kent 1984, Lucy and McCracken 1985, and McCracken 1985).

[9] It should be noted that the "basswood" connection is not peculiar to the Niagara region alone. Fenton (1940: 229) indicates that the large Seneca village at Boughton Hill was known to some Mohawk as *Kohoseraghe*, "basswood place," and the surrounding area was known as the place with "basswood bark lying around."

ETHNOGRAPHIC COMPARISONS

The bark canoes luted with gum used by the Massawomeck (Wright and Freund 1953: 108; Barbour 1969: 361) contrast sharply with the dugout canoes used by the tidewater Algonquians. George Percy in his *Discourse* (Barbour 1969: 134) describes Algonquian dug-out canoes fortyfive feet long which had been made from a whole tree. In his *True Relation* (1608: 358) Smith notes some canoes were " . . . an elne deep and 40 to 50 foot in length and some will bear 40 men but the most ordinary are smaller and will bear 10, 20, or 30 . . . ." Spelman's account of the Massawomeck using dug-out canoes ca. 1609 in their war with the Potomeck (Smith 1624: 33; Arber 1884: cxiv; Tooker 1894: 184; Hoffman 1964: 199) appears to reflect a Massawomeck readiness to use captured Algonquian dug-out canoes which would be better than their Iroquoian elmbark equivalents.

Close reading of Fleet's account of the use "birchen canoes" on the Potomac in 1632 (Neill 1876: 26) will reveal that these were used by the Piscataway, not the Massawomeck. However, it seems likely that these canoes had been obtained by the Piscataway from a group farther north, possibly the Massawomeck, as a result of their fur trading activities.

In his *Map of Virginia* (Barbour 1969: 361) Smith notes that Massawomeck " . . . Targets [shields], Baskets, Swords, Tobacco-pipes, Platters. Bowes and Arrowes and everything they showed" were much superior, he says "much exceeded," to those used by Chesapeake Bay Algonquians. Although these comparisons set Massawomeck artifacts apart from the tidewater Algonquians, the information is insufficient to permit a significant conclusion regarding the identity of the Massawomeck.

ARCHAEOLOGICAL EVIDENCE

At present, and apart from certain artifacts excavated in connection with known European settlements, installations, and habitation sites, the European material from Indian archaeological sites which can be attributed to the sixteenth century and the first quarter of the seventeenth century, still cannot be identified, unequivocably, as having been introduced by the nationals of a specific European country. Nor can the European material excavated from Indian sites be attributed, with certainty, to a documented event when Europeans are known to have introduced European material into the Indian community, or are known to have been in the company of Indians in the region. Consequently it is not possible, at present, to provide evidence which can, with reasonable certainty, be used to demonstrate the direction from whence came the European material excavated.

No archaeological sites have been identified which can be attributed to the Massawomeck. Indeed, until a territory can be attributed to them, it does not appear likely that specific sites can be investigated to ascertain whether they can be attributed to the Massawomeck. Until this can be done it will not be possible to compile criteria against which to compare and contrast Massawomeck archaeological data with those of other Iroquoian groups. Nevertheless there are aspects of the Jamestown settler's accounts regarding their relations with the Indians which are manifested in current archaeological data.

Strachey's remarks regarding the large quantity of English axes in the Indian community by 1608 are borne out by existing Susquehannock archaeological data. The twenty-four iron axes excavated at the Washington Boro site, a Susquehannock early historic village dated ca. 1600–1625 (Kent 1984: 292), represents a five-fold increase in the incidence of these European tools over those from the nearby Schultz site dated ca. 1575–1600, which is believed to be the next earliest site in the Susquehannock archaeological sequence. The quantity of European goods excavated on the Washington Boro site is not exceeded until the mid-seventeenth century when fifty-three axes appear on the historic Strickler site which is attributed to the period 1645–1665 (ibid.).

Archaeological data from farther afield, although sometimes more oblique, are germane in this context. The thin scattering of European iron and brass excavated on early Seneca and Onondaga protohistoric sites closely resembles the situation on early protohistoric Susquehannock sites in Bradford County. This similarity has been remarked upon by Heisey and Witmer (1962: 108), Kinsey (1969: 67), and Bradley (1979: 379) who have attributed this patterning of European material on protohistoric Iroquois sites to the last half of the sixteenth century. Bradley (ibid.: 380) also explains how on " . . . 16th century Onondaga sites a correspondence exists between the increasing presence of European goods and a growing influence of southern [in part Susquehannock] traits." He elaborates on this relationship in his recent work *The Evolution of the Onondaga* (1987: 60, 90, 96–99, 103). Nevertheless, it remains to be demonstrated whether these Seneca and Onondaga obtained this material with southern traits by preying directly on Chesapeake Bay Algonquians and the Susqhenannock or whether they obtained it from middlemen who had received it from these tidewater people. Like all Five Nation Iroquois, the Seneca and Onondaga were located on or near the headwaters of the Susquehanna River at this time, so they were in regions in which the terrain provided best access to the Susquehannock villages in the Susquehanna River valley, however hostile their reception might have been. Possibly the Massawomeck, who certainly did intervene at tidewater, played some intermediary role in the introduction of European goods and marine shell to the Five Nation Iroquois, at least to those Iroquois with whom they were allied, ca. 1615, but this has not been demonstrated.

V. HYPOTHESES

This work demonstrates the elasticity of the confusion which sometimes occurs when different European observers refer to the same group of Indians, often at different times and in different places, using different names. Here we have on one hand John Smith, an Englishman in Virginia in 1608, using mid-Atlantic Algonquian information and names to describe a group of Indians, and on the other hand we have Champlain, a Frenchman in Huronia in 1615, using Iroquoian information and names, specifically Huron-dialect Iroquoian, to describe the same group of Indians.

Discussion cannot but arise regarding the possibility that there were Massawomeck elements, possibly those peripheral to the main group, whose "history" might not be wholly congruent with the hypothesis proferred here. Certainly experience with better-known Iroquoian groups suggests that this would not be unusual. Unfortunately the scope and nature of the primary and contemporary sources on which this work is premised, perforce, does not permit a discussion *based on evidence* regarding either the existence of peripheral Massawomeck groups, or how their "history" might vary from the main-line events examined here. To do so on the basis of the evidence extant would, I believe, lead us into a morass of speculation premised on an endless proliferation of 'if' and 'perhaps'. I have opted to explain the evidence extant.

TWO MASSAWOMECK HOMELANDS

Seventeenth-century primary and secondary accounts regarding the Massawomeck indicate that in the period 1607–1634 they occupied two distinct and widely separated territories. Initially ca. 1608 they were located in a lacustrine territory associated with the St. Lawrence River, the "River of Canada," in a manner not yet understood clearly. Later ca. 1632 when they were visited by Edward Fleet, they were located in the Appalachian hinterland not far from Chesapeake Bay remote from the "river of Cannida."

In 1607 Smith learned from Powhatan that the Massawomeck homeland was a riverine or lacustrine territory. In 1608 the Tockwogh and Susquehannock confirmed this location. Although Powhatan had made it clear to Smith in 1608 that the Massawomeck were located on a freshwater lake, Smith continued to describe this as a marine location as late as 1612 (Barbour 1969: 361, 414). Three primary sources[1] independently describe it as on the "river of Cannida" or in "some part of Commada" (op. cit.). Both the early seventeenth-century maps which depict the Massawomeck, the Zúñiga sketch map of ca. 1608 (Fig. 2) and Smith's *Virginia* map of 1612 (Fig. 1), place the Massawomeck in a lacustrine location. William Blaeu's map of 1630 (Portinaro and Knirsch 1987: pl. 74), which is a detailed reproduction of Smith's map *Virginia*, adds nothing new in this regard. Nevertheless, there is not a shred of evidence to suggest that this information was derived from Europeans who visited the Massawomeck homeland during the first decade of the seventeenth century. All the data available regarding this location of Massawomeck territory reflect what the Virginians learned first-hand from widely separated and independent Indian accounts—two Algonkian, Powhatan and Tockwogh, and one Susquehannock Iroquoian.

On the basis of this evidence, it is postulated that ca. A.D. 1607 the Massawomeck were located in the region at the east end of Lake Erie or the west end of Lake Ontario, east of the Niagara River. In either of these locations they would be associated with the "river of Cannida" in the context of the Great Lakes-St. Lawrence River waterway. At this time and in this location they would be in a position to receive European material from the French as the Susquehannock and Tockwogh had related to Smith in 1608. The absence of any French notice of this trade suggests that they obtained French goods through Huron and Neutral middlemen.[2] This is not a new idea. In 1881 Royce (1881: 179, 181), having studied much the same evidence which has been examined here,

[1] In *The Proceedings* Powell and Todkill state the Massawomeck "inhabit the river of Cannida" (Barbour 1969: 408; Quinn 1979 (5): 323). Smith repeated this information in his *Map of Virginia* (Barbour 1969: 361). In 1624 in his *General Historie* Smith stated that the Massawomeck were either from "some part of Commada" or "an inlet on a sea" (1624: 33). Once again Smith has indicated a marine location in spite of the fact that Powhatan had corrected him on this point in 1608. Strachey repeated Smith, placing the Massawomeck in "some part of Caneda, some great lake, or some inlet of some sea that may fall into the West Ocean" (Wright and Freund 1953: 107). It is not certain whether Strachey is here simply ignoring Powhatan's correction regarding the salt-water sea, or was in fact unaware that Powhatan had corrected Smith.

[2] The earliest archaeological evidence of European material among the Ontario Iroquois has been dated to the end of the first quarter of the sixteenth century, although there are claims for some being present as early as the end of the fifteenth century (Noble 1980: 4; Trigger 1976: 449 n 40; 1985: 151). At that time European goods received initially by the Montagnais from French and Basque fishermen on the Gulf of St. Lawrence and in the Strait of Belle Isle were moved northward on St. Lawrence River tributaries in that region to the hinterland Algonquians. In the region where these St. Lawrence River tributary headwaters are adjacent to the headwaters of the Ottawa River, particularly at the headwaters of the St. Maurice River, European goods entered a zone where the Algonquian bands were either in contact with the Huron or with other Algonquian bands, the Nippissing for example, who were in contact with the Huron. As a result of this trading on the hinterland river networks European material became available to the Huron long before Europeans encountered Huron traders on the lower St. Lawrence River in 1609.

From ca. 1580, possibly as early as 1562, French fur traders had been trading in significant numbers on the St. Lawrence River as far up as the Lachine Rapids (LeBlant et Beaudry 1967; Pendergast 1985). While there is no evidence of these Europeans having ascended

suggested that ca. 1608 the Massawomeck homeland was located in the Niagara region.

Evidence regarding the location of the second Massawomeck homeland is more substantial. Edward Fleet visited the Massawomeck territory in 1632, and spent "seven days going and five days comming" back to the Great Falls on the Potomac (Neill 1876: 28). Estimates premised on the length of his journey and a reasonable distance to travel each day led Hoffman (1964: 200–201) to suggest Fleet would have arrived at the headwaters of the North Branch of the Potomac River. Had he crossed the watershed into the Ohio River drainage he would have entered the region in which the headwaters of the Monongehela or the Youghiogheny rivers rise.

Fleet did not place the Massawomeck in a lacustrine location nor did he associate this Massawomeck territory with the "river of Cannida." Indeed, Fleet's account in 1632 stands in sharp contrast to Smith's account in 1608. Now it was the Hereckeenes (Erie), who lived three days journey beyond the *Mosticum* Massawomeck, which carried on a "trade in Cannida" with the French on the St. Lawrence River. On the other hand by 1632 the Massawomeck had turned to Algonquian middlemen on the Potomac River where they had an arrangement which permitted them to have access to the European material being introduced into Chesapeake Bay. Calvert's experience in 1634 emphasizes the importance of this trade to the English and in so doing provides a glimpse of Massawomeck involvement in a wider trade than Fleet describes. His explanation that the Massawomeck "cometh seven, eight, and ten day journey" to trade at the mouth of the Potomac River generally confirms Fleet's location of the Massawomeck homeland, but the travel time, which is in excess of that related by Fleet, suggests that the Massawomeck homeland may have included territories beyond the Potomac River in the Ohio River watershed.

Jansson's map *America Septentrionale* of 1636 (Goss 1990b: 72) is the earliest to place the Massawomeck in the Chesapeake Bay hinterland, a location compatible with accounts by Fleet and Calvert. Dudley's derivative map *Virginia Vecchio è Nuoua* of 1647, which has been described as one of the best maps of Virginia in the seventeenth century, also places the Massawomeck in this location. Farrar's map of 1651 (Fig. 4) and the Hondius-Visscher map of 1669 (G. Shilder *World Map of 1669*) (Fig. 6), both of which are largely derivative, also place the Massawo-

the St. Lawrence River beyond the Lachine Rapids in the sixteenth century, there is every likelihood that European goods introduced by these traders at the Lachine Rapids were moved onward to the Ontario Iroquois and the hinterland by the Ottawa River Algonquian allies of the Montagnais on the axis of the Ottawa River and possibly on the axis of the St. Lawrence River. The presence of European goods on the latter route has not been demonstrated. In 1626, which is somewhat late in this context, the visit of the Ottawa River Algonquian chieftain *Iroquet* to the eastern villages of the Neutral (Sagard 1636) suggests that there was person-to-person contact between Algonquians located on the lower Ottawa River, not far from the Lachine Rapids, and the Iroquoians at the head of Lake Ontario. Daillon makes it clear that by 1626 French *coureurs de bois* from the Canada region were trading in the region at the head of Lake Ontario with some regularity (Sagard 1636).

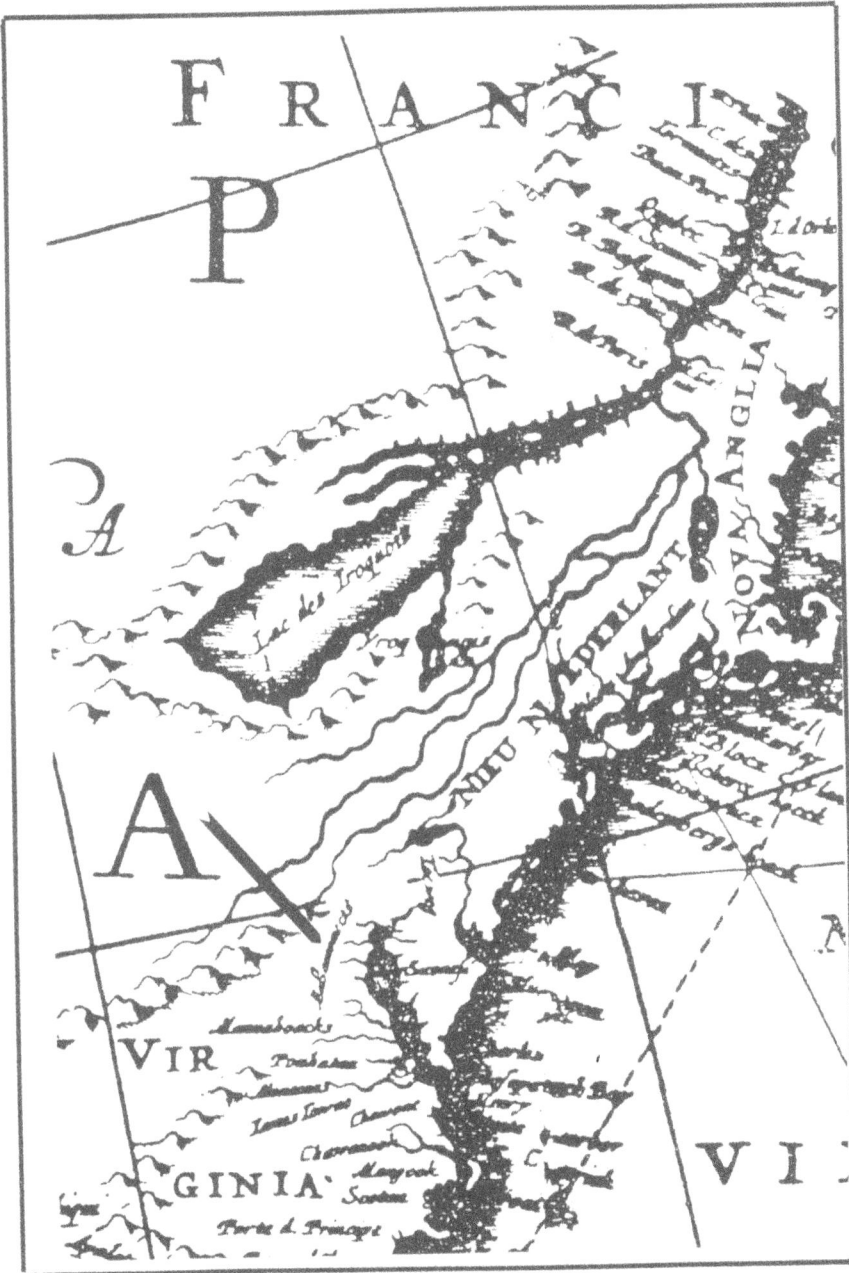

FIG. 6. The Hondius-Visscher map of 1669, *World Map of 1669* by Jodocus Hondius the Elder and Nicholas Visscher, Amsterdam 1978. The *Massawomeck* are located in the hinterland west of Chesapeake Bay.

meck in an Appalachian hinterland. Lederer's note on his 1672 map (Fig. 5) that "The Massawomeck dwelt heretofore beyond these mountains" is the last reference to the Massawomeck on a contemporary map. The location of the Massawomeck on the wholly derivative Delisle map of ca. 1700 simply reflects this and earlier information. Neither Lord Baltimore's earlier English map *Noua Terrae-Mariae* of 1635, revised by John Ogilby in 1671 (Cumming 1982: 288) nor William Blaeu's earlier Dutch map *Nova Belgica et Anglia Nova* of 1635 (ibid.: 284) indicate a location for the Massawomeck or the Antouhonorons, although the latter incorporates, severely distorted, the St. Lawrence River and the Lake Ontario regions.

On the basis of this evidence, it is postulated that by ca. 1627 the Massawomeck homeland was located in the hilly Appalachian hinterland in the region between the headwaters of the North Branch of the Potomac River and the headwaters of the Youghiogheny River. Here between Lake Erie and Chesapeake Bay the Massawomeck were adjacent to and three days journey from the Hereckeene Erie. They were also on, or adjacent to, the headwaters of streams which provided access to Chesapeake Bay where European material was available. There is no evidence that the Massowomeck continued to carry on a trade in marine shell with Algonquians in the Tangier Sound region, from their Appalachian homeland.

IDENTITY OF THE MASSAWOMECK

It is proposed to examine the Indian groups which appear on seventeenth-century maps in the two homeland locations which have been attributed to the Massawomeck by primary and contemporary sources. Champlain's map of 1616 (Fig. 7), which is the first to depict the interior beyond the foot of Lake Ontario (Wroth 1952: 2), provides the earliest record of people between lakes Ontario and Erie in the region east of the Niagara River. There, in an understandably distorted representation of the local geography, Champlain places the *Antou-honorons*. This map, which was published in 1619 to accompany his work *Les Voyages*, incorporates information Champlain had received during the period 1615–1618. As a result his knowledge of the *Antouhonorons* must be attributed to his Indian associates, probably the Huron and the Ottawa River Algonquian *Ononchataronon* and their chief *Iroquet*.

Champlain's map *Carte de la Nouvelle France* of 1632 (Fig. 8) is the next map to depict the region between lakes Ontario and Erie. This map, which represents hinterland geography more accurately, locates the *Antouoronons* (sic) in the region adjacent to Lake Ontario a short distance east of where he placed the *Antou-honorons* on his 1616 map. Apart from *La nation neutre*, which Champlain located on the *south* side of Lake Erie, the remainder of this region is unoccupied. Although Champlain names

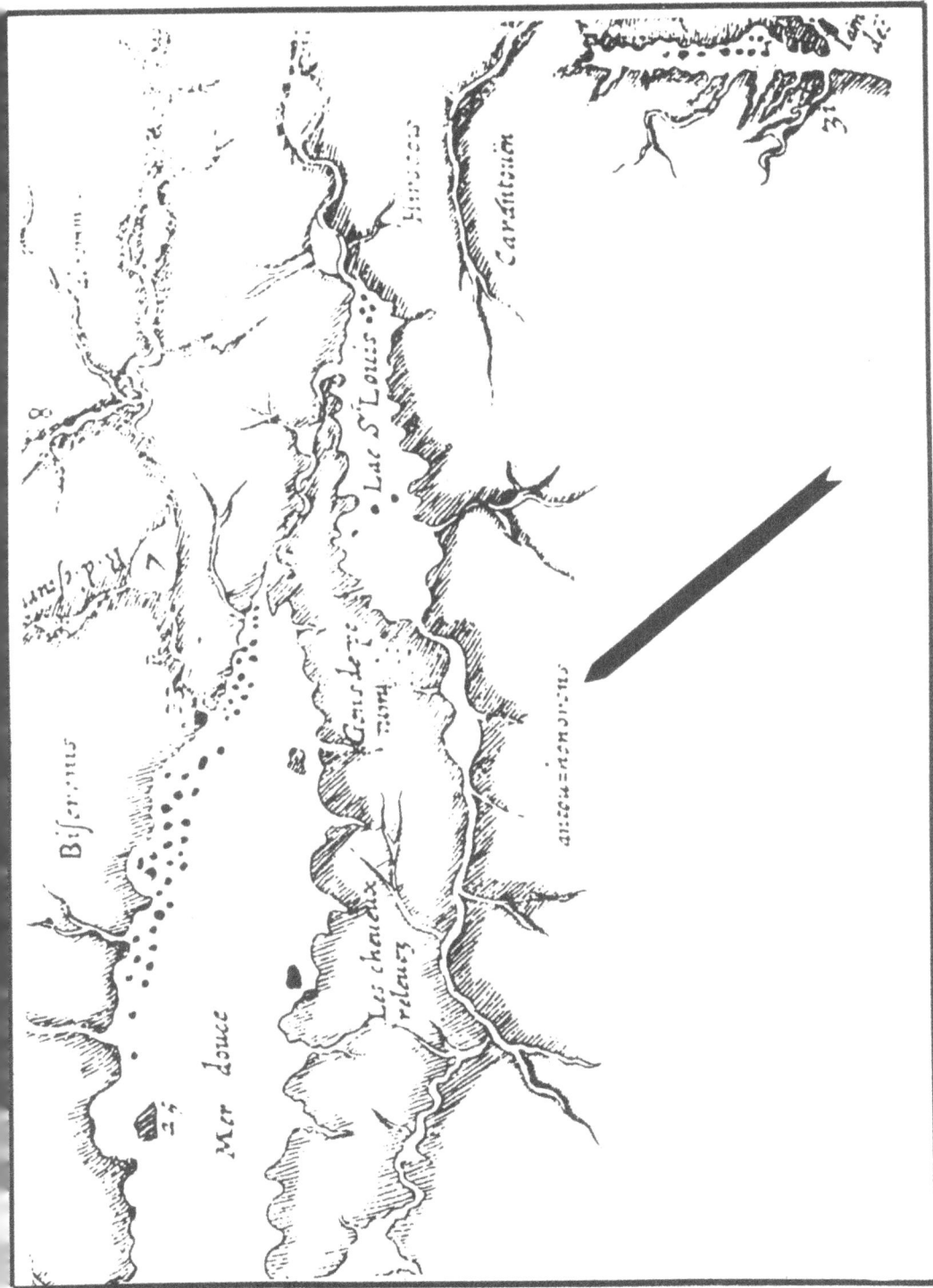

FIG. 7. Champlain's map of 1616. The *Antou-honorons* are located south of an ill-defined Lake Erie.

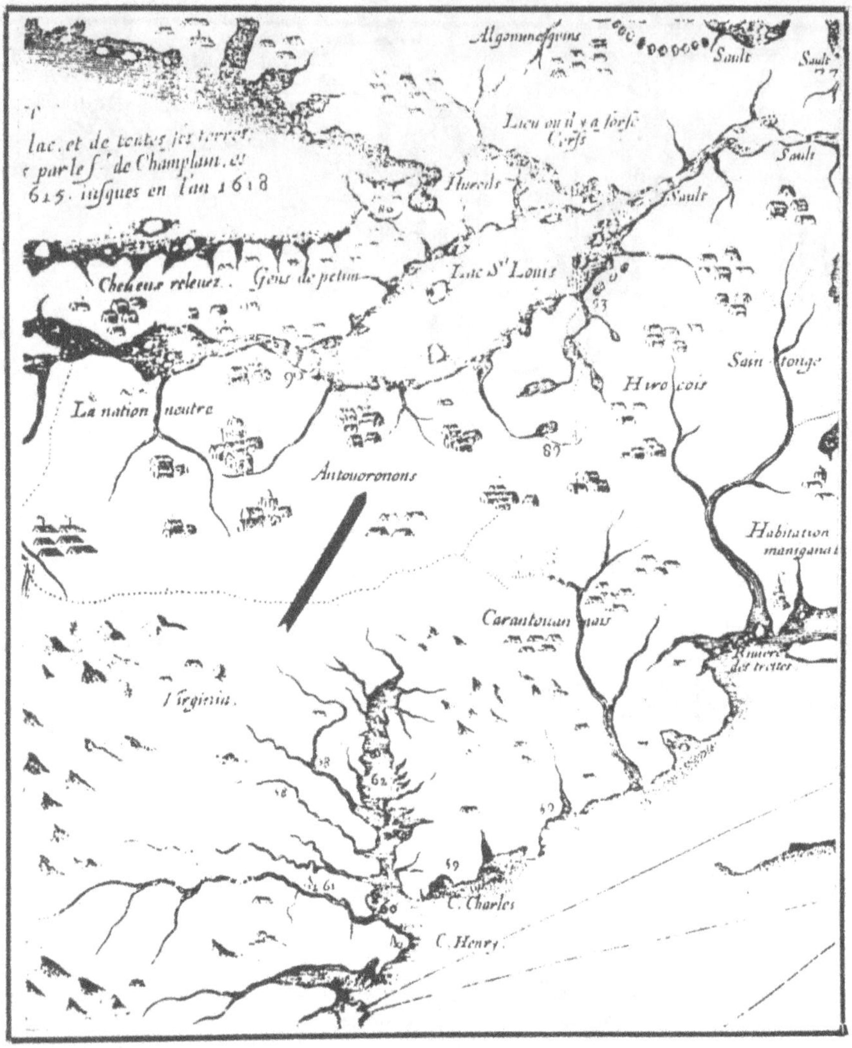

FIG. 8. Champlain's map of 1632. The *Antouoronons* are located south of Lake Ontario east of the Niagara River. Note that Champlain has erroneously located *La nation neutre* south of Lake Erie.

Lake Ontario *Lac St. Louis* on both the 1616 and the 1632 maps, in his explanatory text he refers to it several times as 'the lake of the *Entouhonoron*' (Biggar 1929 (3): 58–59, 62–64, 79) thereby indicating his conviction that the *Antounoron* homeland was in some manner closely associated with Lake Ontario.

The *Nouvelle France* map of ca. 1641 (Fig. 9) has been attributed to Jean Bourdon (Heidenreich 1988) who, having arrived in New France in 1634, visited the Mohawk with Father Jogues in 1646. His duties as clerk of the *Communauté*, which required him to travel extensively to supervise the fur trade (Hamelin 1966), provided him an opportunity to become familiar with the interior. He locates the *Akhrakvaetonon* in the region

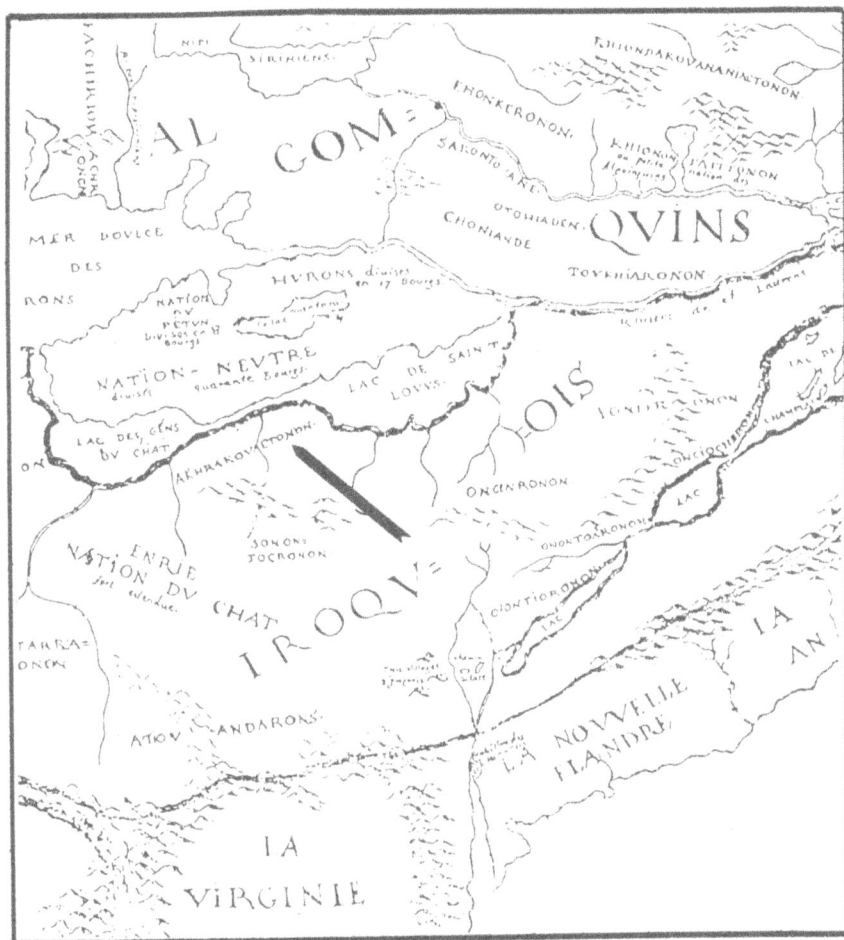

FIG. 9. The c. 1641 map attributed to Bourdon. The *Akhrakvaetonon* have replaced Champlain's *Antouhonorons* in the area east of the Niagara River. Note that the *Nation-Neutre* have been located correctly on the north shore of Lake Erie.

east of the Niagara River between Lake Ontario and Lake Erie. The *Antouoronons* placed in this region on Champlain's maps of 1616 and 1632 do not appear on the Bourdon map. It is interesting to note that the *Nouvelle France* map is the earliest to place the Neutral *north* of Lake Erie.

The Boisseau map *Nouvelle France* of 1643 (Heidenreich 1971: map 6), and the Laigniet and de Fer map *La Nouvelle France* of 1669 (ibid.: map 7), are both derivatives duplicating Champlain's map of 1632 regarding the location and spelling of the *Antouoronons* and *La nation neutre*.[3] Con-

---

[3] The Laigniet and de Fer map of 1669 provides two additional entries in this region: west of the legend *La nation neutre* and adjacent to a waterfall symbol depicting Niagara Falls there appears the entry *St François*; between *Lac St. Louis* (Lake Ontario) and the *Antou(h)onorons* there appears an indistinct entry *N?? des la meangrs* (?).

rad Heidenreich has noted (pers. comm. 1987), that both these maps were printed from Champlain's 1632 copper plate.

The Sanson map *Amérique Septentrionale* of 1650 (White 1978a: 414) locates the *N. Neutre* north of Lake Erie and the *N. du Chat* at the east end and south of Lake Erie, but leaves the region east of the Niagara River unlabeled. As a result neither the *Antou(h)onorons* nor the *Akhrakvaetonon* are indicated. Sanson's map *Le Canada ou Nouvelle France* of 1656 (White 1978a: 415) locates the *Attiou anaarons* beyond the mountains at the headwaters of what appears to be the Appomattox River and again in the region north of Lake Erie as the *Neutre ou Attiouandarons*. The *Eriechronons ou N. du Chat* are located south of Lake Erie. The area east of the Niagara River carries only the caption *Ongiara Sault*. Once again neither the *Antou(h)onorons* nor the *Akhrakvaetonon* are indicated. Heidenreich (pers. comm. 1987) has suggested that the Indian names on the *Le Canada ou Nouvelle France* map are derived from the *Nouvelle France* map of ca. 1641 which has been attributed to Bourdon. Sanson's map *Le Nouveau Mexique et La Florida*, which was also published in 1656, does not include the Neutral but continues to locate the *Eriechronons* south of and at the east end of Lake Erie. The *Ongiara* are placed immediately east of the Niagara River. Neither the *Antou(h)onorons* nor the *Akhrakvaetonon* are mentioned on this map.

Du Val's *Le Canada* map of 1653 (Fig. 10), which is derived from Champlain's of 1616, duplicates exactly Champlain's location and spelling of the *Antouhonorons*. However, in designating the *Nation du Chat* for the first time and placing them correctly on the *south* side of Lake Erie where Champlain had located the Neutral in 1632, Du Val appears to have had access to information which was not available to Champlain in 1616 and 1632. Du Val also correctly locates the Neutral on the north side of Lake Erie.

The Bressani map *Novae Franciae Accurata Delineato* of 1657 (Heidenreich 1971: map 10) locates the *Gens neutre* at the head of Lake Ontario and the *Erie populi* well to the south of Lake Erie. Neither the *Antou(h)onoron* nor the *Akrakvaetonon* are indicated by Bressani.

Du Creux's 1660 map *Tabula Novae Franciae* (Heidenreich 1971: map 11) places the *Gens Neutra* at the head of Lake Ontario but there is no mention of the Erie. An indistinct entry immediately east of the Niagara River appears to read *Ondaeron II On dieromius pagus*. Neither the *Antou(h)onorons* nor the *Akhrakvaetonon* are located on this map.

The map dated ca. 1680 which is attributed to Abbé Claude Bernou (Trigger 1976: 798; White 1978: 408) locates the *Antouaronons* (sic) on the north shore of Lake Erie together with the information that they were a "nation destroyed." The two symbols which accompany this entry have been interpreted to indicate the Antouaronons once consisted of two villages. The *Akhrakvaetonon* are not shown on this map. It is possible that the location of the *Antouhonorons* on the north side of Lake Erie represents the cartographer's intention to convey the information that

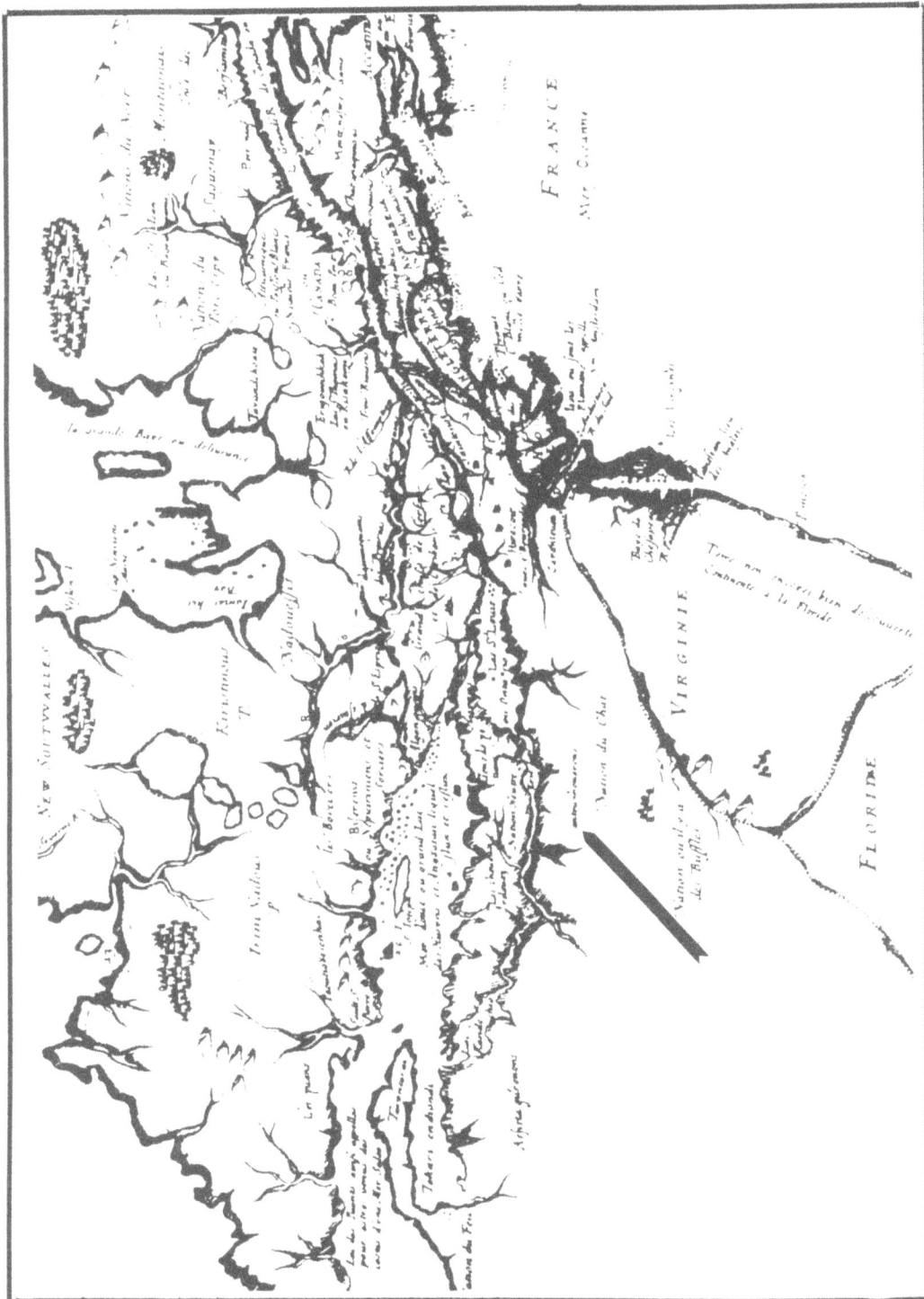

FIG. 10. The Du Val Map of 1653. Information on the Antouhonorons is identical to that shown on Champlain's map of 1616 from which the Du Val map is derived.

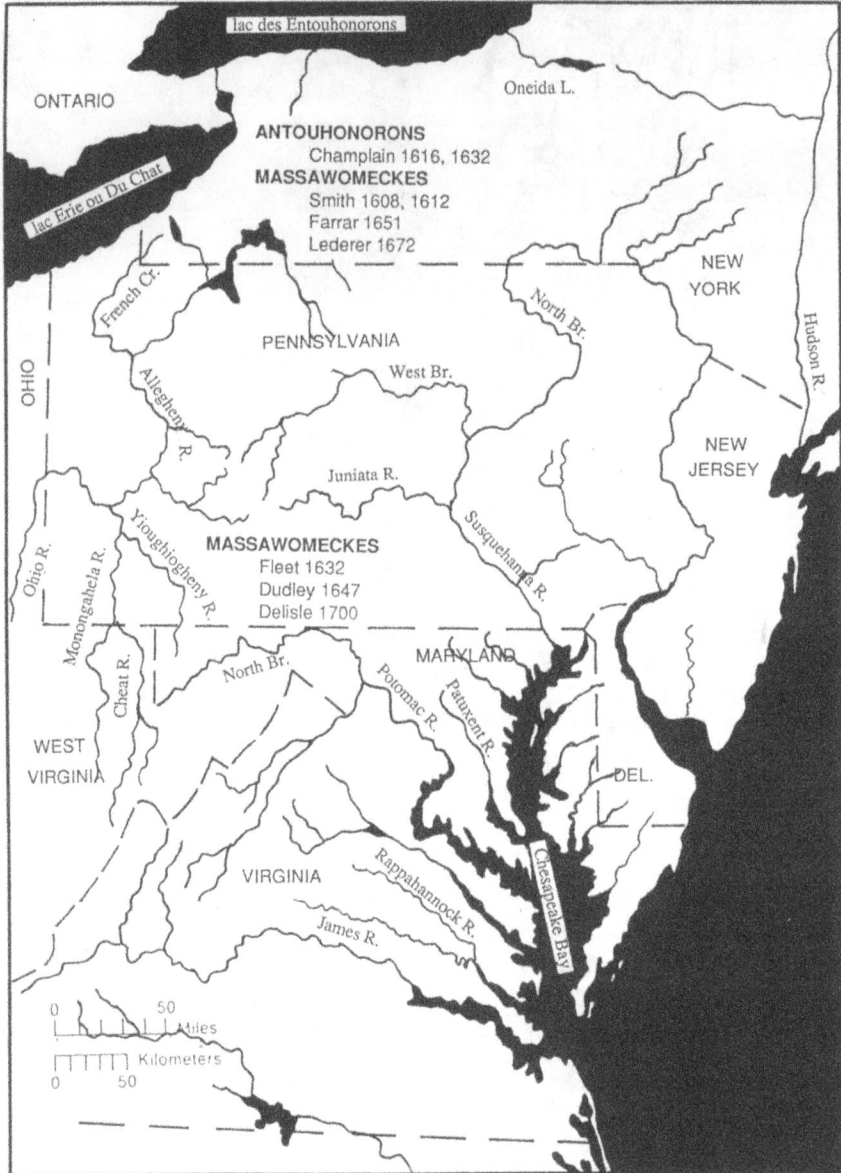

FIG. 11. Modern map showing the homelands attributed to the Antouhonorons and Massawomeckes by seventeenth and eighteenth century sources.

this "nation" had been destroyed as a marginal note on his map, rather than locate precisely a "nation" which was no longer extant. Otherwise this location is an error for this is the only instance in which the *Antouhonoron* are located north of the Great Lakes. The J.B. Louis Franquelin map places the *Antouaronons* south of Lake Erie with the notation that they were a nation destroyed. Both the Bernou and Franquelin maps incorporate material derived from LaSalle's explorations in 1669.

This review of the cartographic evidence indicates that ca. 1608 when Powhatan, the Tockwogh, and the Susquehannock were explaining to John Smith how their mortal enemies, the Massawomeck, lived on the "river of Cannida" in a location compatible with the Niagara Frontier region, contemporary French maps were locating Champlain's *Antouronons* and later Bourdon's *Akhrakvaetonon* in the Niagara River region. The close association of these two groups in this context demands that they be examined in detail.

The Akhrakvaetonon

The *Nouvelle France* map of ca. 1641 attributed to Bourdon contains the only cartographic reference to the *Akhrakvaetonon*, although they appear in contemporary literature several times. They appear first in the list of tribes set out in the *Jesuit Relation* for 1640 (Thwaites 1895–1901 (18): 232), which is believed to have been derived from Rageneau's lost map. Here the *Akhrakvaetonon* appear in the sequence immediately after the *Aondironon* and *Ongmarahronon*, both of which have been attributed to the Neutral (Hodge 1910: 63; White 1978: 411; Steckley 1985: 12) and immediately before the *Oneronon*, which have been identified as Wenro (White 1978: 411; Steckley 1985a: 17). In the 1656 list of tribes (Thwaites 1895–1901 (42): 197) the *Akhrakvaetonon* are mentioned following the *Atiraguenrek* and *Atiaonrek*, both of which the Neutral names (White 1978: 411; Steckley 1985: 12), and before the *Gentuetehronons*, or *Gentaguetehonons*, an Erie group (Hodge 1907: 490; Fenton 1940: 195; White 1978: 412; Steckley 1985: 12). Both these listings place the *Akhrakvaetonon* in a sequence which is believed to reflect the relative geographical location of these groups. This would locate the *Akhrakvaetonon* in the Niagara River region. In the 1740s the *Akhrakvaetonon* were listed after the *eraenrek* or Neutral (Steckley 1985: 12) and before the *Rie* or Erie (ibid.). This too places the *Akhrakvaetonon* in the Niagara River region. While it would be difficult to demonstrate that these three listings constitute independent sources supporting a single location for the *Akhrakveatonon*, they consistently place this group in the Niagara River region, a location which accords well with the Bourdon map. The Boucher

Relation of 1655–1656 (Thwaites 1895–1901 (45): 207) explains that the *Trakwaehrons*, a synonym, are "utter foreigners although they form without doubt the largest and best part of the Iroquois."

Other documentary evidence regarding the *Akhrakvaetonon* has been interpreted differently. An entry in the *Journal des Pères Jésuits* for 4 June, 1652 chronicles, in part, how two Algonquian women who, having escaped from the Mohawk, related: "The Iroquois, having gone during the winter [1651–1652] in full force against the *Atrakwaeronnons Andastoeronnons* had the worst of it" (Thwaites 1895–1901 (37): 105). A later journal entry for 1 July 1652 clarifies which of these nations had been attacked: "The capture of *Atrakwae* by the Iroquois nations of a thousand. They carried off 5 or 6 hundred—chiefly men" (Thwaites 1895–1901 (37): 111).

Fenton (1940: 237) has suggested that *Atrakwae* may refer to *Quadrogue*, the town on Smith's 1612 map near the mouth of the Susquehanna River. Hewitt (1910: 112) was prepared to accept *Atrakwae(y)* as the Conestoga village from which the Iroquois took 500–600 prisoners in 1652 and it was the seat of the *Akhrakvaetonon*, a division of the Conestoga, (ibid.: 658). Hewitt (1910: 336, 657) has also suggested that the *Scahentoarronon* mentioned in the Jesuit list of 1640 (Thwaites 1895–1901 (18): 232), who were the people of Wyoming flats, and the *Gandastogues* or *Andastoerrhonons* mentioned in the Jesuit Relation for 1672 were also Conestoga. Having suggested that the Scahentoarrhonon were *probably*, the Massawomeck, Hewitt raised the possibility of a Akhrakvaetonon/Scahentoarronon/Andastoerrhonon/Conestoga/Massawomeck synonymy.

Jennings (1982: 221) has interpreted references to this battle with the Iroquois to conclude that *Atrakwaeronons* was a synonym for the Susquehannock. Steckley (1985: 13) has interpreted it to indicate that it was the *Akhrakvaetonon*, or *Atrakwae* (Thwaites 1895–1901 (36): 141; (37): 111) in the Huron dialect, and not the *Andasterrhonon* who were destroyed over the winter of 1651–1652. Although the Mohawk are known to have attacked the Andaste that winter, amicable relations between the Andaste and Mohawk in 1655 (Thwaites 1895–1901 (37): 97; Jennings 1968: 23–26; 1978: 365) indicate conclusively that the Andaste were not destroyed at this time. Indeed, if by using the Huron form *Aktrakwae* for the *Akhrakvaetonon*, Steckley (1985: 13) correctly equates the *Akhrakvaetonon* with the Seneca or Cayuga *Kahkwa*, who are recorded on the Bernou maps of ca. 1680 (Trigger 1976: 798, 838; White 1978: 408) as the *Kakouagoga* "a nation destroyed," it is the more likely that it was the *Akhrakvaetonon* who were destroyed over the winter of 1651–1652.

In this context it is interesting to note that the *Relation* of 1655–1656 (Thwaites 1895–1901 (42): 197) does not list any of these groups as having been destroyed by the Iroquois: "I have made you master of the earth and victors over so many Nations: I made you conquer the Hurons, the Tobacco Nation, the Ahondihronons [a branch of the Neutral (Hewitt

1910: 63)], Atiraguenrek ['under the Neutral' (Hewitt 1910: 62)], Atianrek [probably a synonym for Atiraguenrek, the Neutral], Takoulguehronons [otherwise unknown], and Gentaguetehronons [Erie (Hewitt 1910: 490)].''

At this juncture several interpretive options arise regarding *Akhrak-vaetonon* synonymy. Following from Hewitt's conclusion (1910: 658) that the *Scahentoarronon* and *Akhrakvaetonon* were alternative names for the same group, the latter being in the Huron dialect, Trigger (1976: 97) has suggested the possibility that the early chroniclers had subsumed the *Andaste* and the *Scahentoarronon* under the general name *Susquehannock*.[4] Fenton (1940: 232) and Trigger (1976: 97) appear to have embraced with some certainty Hewitt's suggestion that the Scahentoarronon/Akhrak-vaetonon were *probably* Smith's Massawomeckes (Hewitt 1910: 657). Fenton (1940: 232) adds the *Carantouan* to this synonymy although Champlain (Biggar 1936 (6): 249–250) refers to them as separate nations separated by three days' journey.

These interpretations raise serious problems quite apart from the archaeological discrepancies which have been mentioned (see Chap. IV, n. 8). First, it seems unlikely that as *Massawomeckes* of the Scahentoarronon/Akhrakvaetonon/Carantouan/Conestoga/Andaste/Massawomeck component of the Susquehannock could at the same time be the principal and mortal enemy of the same Susquehannock as related to Smith by both the Susquehannock and Tockwogh in 1608 in no uncertain terms. Further, if indeed the Scahentoarronon/Akhrakvaetonon/Conestoga/Andaste/Carantuan/Massawomeck group were located on the Susquehanna River, in the Wyoming Flats area (Hewitt 1910: 657–58), in relatively close proximity to the Susquehannock, as suggested by Fenton (1940: 233–39) and as is implicit in the Hewitt and Trigger interpretations, they do not, in that place, accord well with Susquehannock and Tockwogh explanations regarding the Massawomeck homeland ca. 1608. Overlooking Smith's erroneous interpretations of Powhatan's relation in 1607 which placed the Massawomeck in a marine location be-

---

[4] The Laigniet and de Fer map *La Nouvelle France* of 1669 separates the *Andastocconons qui sont* (?) *porcelaine*, who are located on this map at the headwaters of what is clearly the Potomac River, from the *Susqiquehan??nna* who are located on this map at the head of Chesapeake Bay. The *Andastocchonons qui sont la Porcellaine* are also shown on the Boisseau map of 1643, *Nouvelle France*, in much the same Potomac River location. The Susquehannock are not indicated. Champlain's map of 1632, the DuVal map *Le Canada* of 1653, which closely resembles Champlain's 1632 map, the Boisseau map of 1643, and the Laigniet and de Fer map of 1669 locate the Carantouannais on the upper reaches of the Delaware River. It is planned to examine the implications of an Andaste location on or near the headwaters of the Potomac River very close to the Massawomeck hinterland homeland during the period depicted by these maps, some of which are highly derivative. It is anticipated that this will have a bearing on the current views regarding the Andaste-Scahentoarronon dichotomy of the encompassing term *Susquehannock*. It may also help further define the Scahentaorronon/Akrakvaetonon/Carantouan synonymy.

yond the hinterland mountains, these twice-told first-hand accounts
place the *Massawomeck* in 1608 in a lacustrine location in "some part of
Commada" where they "inhabit the 'river of Cannida'" (op. cit.). If the
Massawomeck homeland was on the "river of Cannida," and they were
known to Fleet as the "Cannyda Indians," it seems unlikely that the
Susquehannock would place them on the Susquehanna River. Indeed,
there is no evidence to suggest that the Susquehanna River was ever
known as the "river of Cannida."

A new hypothesis is required to reconcile these anomalies. It is, therefore, proposed to remove the Massawomeck from the Scahentoarronon/
Akhrakvaetonon/Conestoga/Andaste/Carantouan/Massawomeck synonymy and place them in a location outside the Susquehanna River
watershed in a "river of Cannida" context compatible with Smith's explanations of the Powhatan, Tockwogh, and Susquehannock accounts.
This would not run counter to any sixteenth-century evidence in this
context, nor would the Scahentoarronon/Akhrakvaetonon/Conestoga/
Andaste/Carantouan synonymy be called into question.

On the other hand failure to remove the Massawomeck from the Sca-
hentoarronon/Akhrakvaetonon/Conestoga/Andaste/Carantouan/Mass-
awomeck synonymy would raise even more serious problems when
tested against Fleet's and Calvert's first-hand accounts regarding the
location of the Massawomeck in the period 1627–1634. At that time fully
credible accounts by Fleet and Calvert regarding the Virginia and Maryland fur trade with the Massawomeck and their middlemen on the Potomac River axis (op. cit.) indicate that the Massawomeck were located
on or near the headwaters of the North Branch of the Potomac River,
or, on or near the Youghiogheny River in the Ohio River basin. Neither
of these places accord well with those attributed to the Scahentoarronon/
Akhrakvaetonon/Andaste/Carantouan during the period 1627–1634. It
should be noted that these observations are wholly independent of the
polemic regarding Andaste and Susquehannock synonymy.

The Antouhonorons

The other Indian group located in the Niagara region ca. 1608 are the
Antouhonorons. They first appear when Champlain recounts how in the
Huron village of Cahiaqué in 1615 he learned of a Huron plan to join
their allies the *Carantouan* in an attack on their common enemy the *Entouhonorons* (Biggar 1929 (3): 53–54; 1932 (4): 244). In his account of the
journey to attack the *Entouhonoron* village Champlain mentions the "lake
of the Entouhonorons," Lake Ontario, several times (Biggar 1929 (3):
58–59, 62–64, 79). The remainder of Champlain's account has not yet
served to identify the location of this *Entouhonoron* village with certainty.
Pratt (1976) has demonstrated that the archaeological site at Nichols

Pond, the location which has long been mentioned as being the site of Champlain's attack, is not that location.[5]

The legend on Champlain's map of 1632 identifies a lacustrine location where there was located a "Village surrounded by four palisades, where Sieur de Champlain went to war against the Antouhonorons and took a number of prisoners." The explanatory text for the 1632 map (Biggar 1936 (6): 249–50) states:

"The Antouhonorons comprise 15 villages built in a strong position. They are enemies of all the other nations except the Neutrals. Their country is a fine one, with an excellent climate, lying near River St. Lawrence. This [thus] they prevent all other nations from passing which explains why that river is less frequented.[6] They cultivate and sow their lands."

"The Iroquois and the Antouhonorons make war together on all other nations except the Neutrals."

"The Carantouanis [sic] are a nation settled south of the Antouhonorons in a very beautiful and excellent country where they are strongly established. They are friends with all other nations except the said Antouhonorons, from whom they are distant only three days' journey. . . ."

Earlier Champlain had estimated that the *Carantouan* lived "three long days journey beyond the *Entouhonorons*" (Biggar 1929 (3): 53–54). On another occasion he confirmed this estimate stating that the *Carantouan* lived "three good days journey beyond the *Entouhonorons*" (Biggar 1932 (4): 244). In 1615 when Champlain dispatched Brulé to make contact with the *Carantouan* in preparation for their attack on the *Entouhonoron's*

---

[5] The location of the Antouhonoron village attacked by Champlain has long been the subject of much discussion. For years the principal contender has been Nichol's Pond near Oneida Lake as General Clark suggested, although sites on Onondaga Lake, Cayuga Lake, and Canandaigua Lake have also been suggested. Fenton (1940: 213-16) has remarked that, "until someone demonstrates that there is a suitable site on the east shore of Onondaga lake, the proponents of Gen. John S. Clark's old theory, which favours the Nichols Pond site, have offered the only concrete evidence." In his *Archaeology of the Oneida Iroquois*, Pratt (1976) has compiled a comprehensive review of the documentary and archaeological evidence having a bearing on the location and identification of the Entouhonoron village Champlain attacked. Cogently he has concluded (ibid. 148), "Examination of the natural setting, historical documents and maps and of the archaeological record clearly show that Nichols Pond [an Oneida archaeological site] was *not* the site of Champlain's battle in 1615. James Bradley plans to examine an archaeological site which, judging from the surrounding terrain, appears more likely to be the correct location (pers. comm. October 1988).

[6] Champlain can only have known the location of the Antouhonorons in a lacustrine setting at the head of the "lake of the Entouhonoronos," from the Indians or the *coureurs de bois*. Both these groups would understand the geography of an extended Great Lakes-St. Lawrence River waterway which underlies Champlain's garbled explanation. Antouhonoron domination of the Niagara River, which seems likely, could inhibit the use of that waterway by groups in that region and so, by extension, their entry into the St. Lawrence. There is no case for placing the Antouhonoron at the east end of Lake Ontario to be able better to prevent other nations from using the St. Lawrence River. In that location they would be in St. Lawrence Iroquoian territory, where long before 1615 the inhabitants of this region had been destroyed.

village, Champlain instructed him ". . . to go towards the Entouhonorons *at* Carantouan" (d'aller vers les Entouhonorons à Carantouan)
(Biggar, 1929 (3): 213–40), thereby raising the possibility that they were
collocated or nearly so. Beauchamp (1895: 321) had earlier suggested
that the *Carantounnais* and the *Antouhonarons* (sic) were enemies.

Apart from these cartographic and locational references, the *Entou-
honoron* are not often mentioned in the literature. When Champlain
spent the winter of 1615–1616 in Huronia he interceded on behalf of the
Algonquian chief *Iroquet* in a dispute regarding the disposition of an
Entouhonoron prisoner who had been captured during the attack in 1615
(Biggar 1929 (3): 99–100, 111; 1932 (4): 283). A Neutral alliance with the
Antouhonoron, which excluded the Huron, was demonstrated when
Champlain attempted to visit the Neutral in the winter of 1615. The
Huron prevented him from making this journey claiming that it would
not be safe because they had incurred Neutral displeasure when in 1614
they had killed a Neutral while attacking the *Entouhonorons*. Here we
have confirmation, or repetition, of the 1632 map legend regarding the
Antouhonoron-Neutral alliance.

Although the *Antouhonorons* are mentioned in the *Jesuit Relations* some
twenty-five times by this and various other spellings, they are not included as *Antouhonorons* in Brebeuf's list of tribes set out in Le Jeune's
Relation of 1635 (Thwaites 1895–1901 (8): 115–117). Neither are they mentioned in the *Relation* of 1640 which lists the tribes derived from Rageneau's lost map (Thwaites 1895–1901 (18): 232), nor are they mentioned
in subsequent lists of tribes (Thwaites 1895–1901 (42): 197). Thwaites does
not mention them in his extensive notes on the Iroquoian tribes
(Thwaites 1895–1901 (8): 297–302) nor are they included in Hodge's
Handbook (1910).

Several scholars have sought to equate the *Antouhonorons* (Entouhonorons) with one or another of the Five Nation Iroquois tribes. This is
surprising because Champlain's text explaining his 1632 map clearly
differentiates between them. He states, "The Iroquois and the Antouhonorons together make war against all other nations" (Biggar 1936 (6):
250) thereby describing two components of a single military alliance.
Neither do any of the Jesuit appellations used for the "Iroquois" or for
the Seneca, Cayuga, Onondaga, Oneida, or Mohawk in the *Jesuit Relations* approximate *Antouhonorons*, or one of its various spelling
(Thwaites 1895–1901 (8): 115–17; (18): 233–35). Nevertheless this did not
deter Parkman (1865: 402–403, n 1), Clark (ibid.), Shea (1878: 107), or
Marshall (1887) from attributing the *Entouhonoron* village attacked by
Champlain to the Onondaga. Later several scholars accepted this Onondaga identification (Biggar 1929 (3): 125; Ganong *in* Biggar 1936 (6): 250;
Fenton 1940: 213, 216, 235; Bishop 1948: 356). Ganong had earlier identified them as Seneca (ibid.: 245). Aptly Trigger (1976: 311) has noted
that "Biggar [1929 (3): 54, 125; 1932 (4): 304] and his co-workers have

led many readers astray by their unwarranted substitution of Onondaga for Entouhonoron in their translations of Champlain's writings." The error had been Parkman's sixty-odd years earlier.

Laverdière (1870: 33–34), Thwaites (1895–1901 (8): 293 n 21; (12): 293; (72): 322) and Hodge (1912 (2): 191–92) suggest that the *Antouhonoron* were Seneca. Because the *Antouhonorons* once moved their villages forty or fifty leagues, Shea (1870: 28 n 2, 83 n 2) suggests that they may be the Wenro who moved to Huronia ca. 1638. Beauchamp (1900: 88) concluded they were Oneida.

Hunter (1959: 10) remarks parenthetically that the Entouhonorons were ". . . probably the Seneca or western Iroquois," presumably meaning the Seneca and Cayuga. Zeller (1962: 28, 36) has suggested, without providing an explanation, that Champlain included the Oneida, Onondaga, Cayuga, and Seneca in the *Entouhonoron*. Trigger too (1976: 227) speculates that *Entouhonoron* was "a term which appears to mean the four western Iroquois tribes," that is all the Five Nations except the Mohawk. Pratt (1976: 55) suggests that *Entouhonoron* was a general term which encompassed the Seneca, Cayuga, and Onondaga. He speculates (ibid.) that there having been a Neutral killed in 1614 by the Hurons when they made war on the *Entouhonorons*, it appears likely that the *Entouhonorons* were the Cayuga or the Seneca whose territories were adjacent to, or not far distant from, the Neutral. Campisi (1976: 490) believed *Antouhonoron* and *Entouhonoron* were Huron dialect names for the Oneida explaining, "however it is unclear whether this term was applied solely to the Oneida or to other Iroquois tribes as well." White (1972: 70) notes the location of the *Antouaronons* (sic) on the Sanson map of 1656, the Bernou map of 1680, and the Franquelin map of 1684 and says that they were a group for "which there is almost no information." Later (1974: 71) she identified the *Antouaronons* with several other groups as distinct subdivisions of the Neutral Confederacy. She notes the spurious location of the *Antouaronons* on the north side of Lake Erie on the Bernou map of 1680 suggesting that later they had moved to the south side of Lake Erie into Erie County to escape the Iroquois. In her definitive paper "Neutral and Wenro" (1978: 411) she notes the location of the *Antouhonorons* on the Bernou map of 1680 and the Franquelin map of 1684 remarking that they ". . . probably refer to the Neutral tribe." White does not mention the Antouhonorons by that name or any of its synonyms in her major works (*Iroquois Culture History in the Niagara Frontier Area of New York State* (1961) and *Ethnic Identification and Iroquois Groups in Western New York and Ontario* (1971). Her advice (1972: 70) that the appearance of the *Antouhonorons* on the Bernou map of 1680 "would appear to be the earliest record of the name *Antouaronons* [sic]" and that "This name is not found in the written accounts" (1978: 411) overlooks Champlain's accounts (op. cit.). Conrad Heidenreich includes an assessment of Entouhonoron identity in his definitive monograph on

Champlain's cartography, *Explorations and Mapping of Samuel de Champlain, 1603–1632*. He suggests that the Entouhonoron village attacked by Champlain was a Cayuga village (Heidenreich 1976: 39–40).

Roy Wright (1974: 85–85) has raised an interesting question regarding the Erie which is germane in the context of this work.

Beginning with Sagard, the chroniclers repeatedly say that "we" or "our Frenchmen" [when they] call the Eries the Nation of (the) Cat(s) (Sagard 1632: 307). The fact that another tribe is simply "named. . . " or "called" may simply reflect its non-French name, but why would precisely one of the few unseen tribes [by the French] receive such a name, and especially why, in this case, should the explanatory translation (which quickly predominates over the native term, indicating greater familiarity of use) be preceded by the indication that *we* use it?

Cogently Wright (ibid.) goes on to note how in 1632, the "seven lusty men in strange attire" who arrived at Great Falls purporting to be *Mostikum* Massomacks, were in fact *Hereckeenes* who lived three days beyond the Massawomeck. They "were not the friends" of the Massawomecks (Neill 1876: 30–31). Gatschett (1881: 322–24) and Wright (ibid.) have identified these *Hereckeenes* as Erie. This synonymy is not known to have been suggested elsewhere.

Recently Steckley (1985: 9–13), in a paper which examines the Antouahonaron/Scahentoarrhonon/Andoouanchronon relationship, has suggested that the latter designation is a copying error. Apart from being listed in the 1640 *Relation* (Thwaites 1895–1901 (18): 232–33) the name *Andoouanchronon* does not appear. If as Steckley suggests (ibid. 11, 13), it was intended to be "something like 'Entoouanronon' it would be acceptable as *Antouahonaron*."

Although the Antouhonorons have been identified as Neutral, or a group of Neutrals (Fenton 1940: 198; White 1974: 71, 1978: 411), Steckley (1985: 18 n 1), having examined the linguistics of several of the names of the Neutral components, states that the *Antouaronon* were not Neutrals. Nevertheless until a satisfactory interpretation is available to explain the significance of the *Attouandarons* being shown twice in widely dispersed areas on the Sanson map of 1656—once as *Neutre ou Attiouadarons* in the southern Ontario region occupied by the Neutral, and once beyond the mountains at the headwaters of what appears to be the Appomattox River—the possibility of an Antouhonoron/Neutral connection should not be rejected. The implications of Champlain's advice that "The Iroquois and the Antouhonorons make war together on all other nations except the Neutrals" cannot but invite scrutiny in this regard.

On the basis of information he received from the Indians, probably Huron or Ononchataronon Algonquians, Champlain recounted how on one occasion the *Antouhonorons* were forced by their enemies to move their villages some forty or fifty leagues (Biggar 1929, (3): 125; 1932, (4): 304). At present the archaeology of the Seneca and Cayuga (Wray 1973;

White, Engelbrecht, and Tooker 1978; Abler and Tooker 1978; Niemczycki 1984; Wray et al 1987), the Oneida (Pratt 1976), and the Onondaga
(Tuck 1971; Bradley 1987) does not indicate any of these tribes moved
any of their villages at any time during the seventeenth century any-
where near the forty or fifty leagues described by Champlain. Unless it
can be demonstrated that one of the Five Nation Iroquois moved a village
this distance in the first quarter of the seventeenth century, it seems
unlikely that a Five Nation tribe can be identified as the Antouhonorons.

From this record two conclusions germane to this thesis emerge. Circa
1616 a portion of the region which lies between Lake Ontario and Lake
Erie east of the Niagara River was occupied by the *Antouhonoron* and
the *Akhrakvaetonon*. It is not clear whether these are the names of two
distinct groups or synonyms for a single group.

Apart from their having been destroyed by the Iroquois over the winter of 1651–1652, there is no additional primary or contemporary evidence regarding the *Akhrakvaetonon*. On the other hand there are accounts associated with the *Antouhonoron* over the period from ca. 1615
to some time before 1627. Having remarked on how the Iroquois periodically move their villages ". . . one, two or three leagues from the
former spot, if they are not forced by their enemies to decamp and move
a greater distance" (Biggar 1929 (3): 125; 1932 (4): 304), Champlain then
goes on to relate twice how on one occasion the *Entouhonorons* were
forced by their enemies to move some forty to fifty leagues,[7] a distance
of 190–250 kilometers or some 120–150 miles, depending on the length
of Champlain's league.

It is postulated that the *Antouhonoron* moved southward to a new
location forty or fifty leagues from their homeland east of the Niagara
River, to an area on or near the Youghiogheny River, an Ohio River
tributary, or possibly to the headwaters of the North Branch of the Potomac River. In either region they would be located near where Fleet
and Calvert located the *Massawomeck* over the period ca. 1627 to 1634.
While English and French maps place the *Massawomeck* in this hinterland
Chesapeake Bay region, none place the *Antouhonoron* there. The groups
which are located in these hinterland Chesapeake Bay regions on contemporary French maps are the *Atiovandarons* on the Bourdon map of
1641 and the *Attiouandarons* on the Sanson map of 1656. However out
of place in this location they may be according to current orthodoxy,
these are names associated with the Neutral. Nevertheless, this connection of the Antouhonorons and Massawomeck with the Neutral in

---

[7] Champlain's *league* has been variously estimated or calculated as being 2.97, 3.07, 3.12,
3.51, and 3.52 miles. It has also been suggested that it was the distance traveled on foot
in one hour. In that event Champlain consistently moved at a faster pace than did infantry
on paved roads in World War II. At that time 2.5 miles in one hour, which included a ten
minute break, was the norm, apart from forced or run-walk "speed" marches. Pratt (1976:
57) has examined these variations in Champlain's *league*, and their implications regarding
the identification of Nichols Pond as the site of Champlain's attack on the Antouhonorons.

a manner not yet clear fits well with Champlain's twice repeated explanation that, "The Iroquois and the *Antouhonorons* make war together on all other nations except Neutral," and the Huron account of how in 1614 while attacking the Entouhonrons they had accidently killed a Neutral then allied (op. cit.).

In consequence, it is postulated that the Iroquoians, who were known to the French as the *Antouhonorons* and to the English as the *Massawomeck*, lived in a location in the region east of the Niagara River prior to 1627 from where they raided and traded with tidewater Algonquians on Chesapeake Bay and its tributaries as related to John Smith in 1607 and 1608. From their homeland in the Niagara region the Massawomeck carried on a trade with their Iroquoian neighbors in European goods and marine shell, particularly *Busycon laeostomum*, which they obtained by raiding and trading in the Chesapeake Bay region before ca. 1627 (Pendergast 1989).

Sometime prior to 1627, how long cannot be stated with certainty, enemies forced the *Antouhonorons* to move from their homeland in the Niagara region to a hinterland location on or near the headwaters of the Youghiogheny River, or to the headwaters of the North Branch of the Potomac River. There as the *Massawomeck* Champlain's *Antouoronons* carried on a fur trade with the English of Chesapeake Bay over the period ca. 1627 to 1634 as related by Gookin, Fleet, and Calvert.

VI. MODEL

From this uneven, confused, often frustrating, record of primary and contemporary accounts, and the accumulation of scholarly opinion over the past hundred years or more, there emerges a body of information which, with varying degrees of credibility, consistently supports a hypothesis that during the period ca. 1607 to 1634 the Antouhonorons/Massawomeck were essentially the same people. The model proposed here, which purports to describe events in this period, is based on this hypothesis.

Circa 1607 the *Antouhonorons*, a populous Iroquoian tribe, lived between lakes Ontario and Erie in the region east of the Niagara River. They were allied to other Iroquoians there and, together with these Iroquois allies, the Antouhonorons made war on all other tribes in the region except the Neutral. For some time prior to 1607 they regularly harassed the Susquehannock Iroquoians on the lower reaches of the Susquehanna River and the Nanticoke, Conoy, and Powhatan Algonquian bands on Chesapeake Bay. These Antouhonoron Iroquoians were known to the Chesapeake Bay Algonquians as Massawomeckes and it is by this Algonquian name that they became known to the English settlers at Jamestown soon after they arrived in 1607.

The Massawomeck/Antouhonorons journeyed from their homeland in the Niagara region to Chesapeake Bay by way of the Allegheny, Monongahela/Youghiogheny, and Potomac rivers. They entered the Bay from the middle reaches of the Potomac River by way of the numerous small rivers which drain the west shore of Chesapeake Bay between the Patuxent and Susquehanna rivers. As a result of their frequent hostile incursions the tidewater end of this invasion corridor was uninhabited. The Potomac and Pawtuxent bands which were adjacent to the southern edge of this corridor were particularly prone to attack by the marauding Massawomeck.

The Susquehannock had come into possession of European goods in small quantities ca. 1550 when they were located on the Susquehanna River near its junction with the Chemung River. Subsequently they moved southward to the lower reaches of the Susquehanna River in the vicinity of present-day Lancaster, Pennsylvania, in part to be closer to a growing source of European material which had been traded into Chesapeake Bay since 1546, possibly earlier. Sometime before 1608 when on the lower Susquehanna River, these Susquehannock came under heavy attack by the Massawomeck/Antouhonoron who raided their heavily fortified villages in search of European goods.

69

The Nanticoke Tockwogh Algonquian band at the head of the Chesapeake Bay on the Sassafrass River, who had by 1608 come under the suzerainty of their powerful and more numerous Susquehannock Iroquoian neighbors, also possessed significant quantities of European goods. As a result they were a target of the Massawomeck/Antouhonoron marauders. Indeed the Massawomeck canoe party encountered by John Smith on Chesapeake Bay on 26 or 27 July 1608 had just raided the Tockwogh village on the Sassafras River and their wounded indicate the ferocity of this encounter. Seemingly the Massawomeck raiders were happier attacking the weaker Algonquian bands than they were engaging the more populous heavily fortified villages of the Susquehannock Iroquois, at least on this occasion.

The Massawomeck/Antouhonoron were not hostile to all Algonquians on Chesapeake Bay. Unlike their Tockwogh cousins to the north who reacted with hostility to the Massawomeck as befitted their status as a client-band under Susquehannock Iroquoian suzerainty, and the Algonquians under Powhatan's suzerainty, the Nanticoke bands on the east shore of Chesapeake Bay south of Tangier Sound on the Delmarva Peninsula had reached an accommodation with the Massawomeck. By 1608 they had become an amicable Massawomeck/Antouhonoron source of European material and marine shell, particularly the marine whelk *Busycon laeostomum* which is peculiar to these latitudes.

European material and marine shell gleaned by the Massawomeck/Antouhonorons raiding and trading into Chesapeake Bay returned with them to their homeland in the Niagara region. Some of the material was later distributed farther afield in the Iroquoian hinterland by ritualistic gift-giving and trade. The exotic value of these materials as gifts in the traditional Iroquois practice of ritualistic gift-giving cannot but have been enhanced in regions far from their source on Chesapeake Bay. The Neutrals, the only nation apart from their Iroquois allies with whom the Massowomeck were not at war, were favored in the distribution of these goods. Subsequently some of the material received by the Neutral, both European goods and marine shell, were traded onward to the Petun and Huron. The presence of *Busycon laeostomum* from the Chesapeake Bay latitudes, both intact shells and artifacts made from fragments, which has long been known from contemporary Neutral, Petun, and Huron archaeological sites in Ontario, particularly in ossuaries, provides striking evidence of this ancient trade. The archaeological data demonstrate a vast increase in the marine shell traded into southern Ontario between 1600 and 1620.

By 1627 there had been a major change in the nature of Massawomeck/Antouhonoron activity in the Chesapeake Bay region. No longer were they marauders periodically pillaging Susquehannock and tidewater Algonquian villages in search of European goods. Around 1627 they had successfully completed a punitive attack on the Conoy Piscataway band on the Potomac River and established suzerainty over the Anacostank pressing them into service to convey them ". . . all such English truck

as commeth into the [Potomac] river." Later in 1632 the Massawomeck/
Antouhonoron met Virginian fur traders at the Great Falls on the Potomac where they negotiated a trading arrangement with the English
which bypassed their Anacostank middlemen.

By 1632, possibly as early as 1627 but after 1622 when the Virginian
fur trade on the Potomac river was confined to the "non-beaver" Indians, the Massawomeck/Antouhonoron had moved from their homeland in the Niagara region to a hinterland Appalachian location west of
Chesapeake Bay from which they were better able to conduct their fur
trade on the Potomac with the Jamestown settlers. The alliance between
the Antouhonoron and the Iroquois noted by Champlain to be in effect
ca. 1615 had ceased to exist before ca. 1627 and new hostilities forced
them to move from their Niagara region homeland. Their move closer
to Chesapeake Bay reflects, in part, their desire to exploit their earlier
ability to obtain European material in this region. There is no evidence
that they continued to trade marine shell from the Tangier Sound region
after they moved to this hinterland. The hostilities which forced the
Antouhonoron/Massawomeck from the region between lakes Erie and
Ontario east of the Niagara River prior to 1627 may be a harbinger of
the unrest in that region which later caused the Wenro to move to Huronia before 1638 and the *Kahkwas* and Erie to be destroyed.

An English eyewitness account of the Massawomeck/Antouhonoron
homeland west of Chesapeake Bay indicates they were a populous "nation" said to number some 30,000, significantly more than the 5,000 tidewater Algonquians estimated by Smith in 1608. They were ruled by
four kings[1] who were allied in some manner as a "confederate nation."

---

[1] Smith indicates on his *Virginia* map of 1612 (Fig. 1) the Massawomecke had *three*
"kings" houses, presumably one in each of their principal villages. Champlain records in
the legend to his 1632 map that the Antouhonoron had fifteen villages (Biggar 1936 (6):
249). In both instances this information was derived from Indian accounts and reflects the
situation in their homeland in the Niagara region. In 1632 Edward Fleet's eyewitness
account of the Massawomeck homeland in the Chesapeake Bay hinterland states there
were *four* kings and he names the four principal villages in which they resided. Fleet also
states that he visited thirty large Massawomeck villages (Neill 1876: 27-28), although that
seems incredible in view of his short stay with the Massawomeck.

Lacking additional information in this regard, and taking these estimates at face value,
it does not seem credible to attribute this significant increase in population over a twenty-
odd year period to an explosion in the Massawomeck birth-rate. On the contrary it seems
likely that, apart from whatever misfortunes they might have encountered, the hostilities
which drove the Massawomeck from their homeland in the Niagara region would result
in a population decrease. Possibly the apparent population increase took place when an
unnamed group allied with the Massawomeck in the hostilities mentioned, joined them
when they were forced from the Niagara region. Possibly other groups along the way,
anticipating attack since the Massawomeck had decamped, joined them. Possibly a group
indigenous to the new Massawomeck homeland west of Chesapeake Bay was adopted by
the Massawomeck. Possibly all three of these eventualities took place. There is evidence
of language dissimilarities among the Massawomeck Fleet traded with at Great Falls in
1632 (see n. 3 below). Nevertheless, this upheaval could conceivably have resulted in a
change in the Massawomeck political structure which is reflected in an increase of their
'kings' from three to four.

Their principal towns were *Tonhoga* (Tohoga), *Mosticum, Shaunetowa,* and *Usserahak;* and their four kings also bore these names.[2] In 1632 by an eyewitness account there were thirty 'towns' one of which allegedly contained 300 houses. These towns were palisaded with ". . . great trees and with scaffolds upon the walls." The Algonquians claimed the Massawomeck were cannibals. It is possible there were language differences between the four Massawomeck/Antouhonoron "kingdoms."[3]

In 1632 Massawomeck/Antouhonoron were neighbors of the Hereckeene Erie who lived three days' journey beyond them, probably to the north. At that time the Hereckeenes and the Massawomeck/Antouhonoron were not openly hostile but neither were they friends or allies. This was, in part, a result of their direct competition for the European goods the English were introducing into the fur trade on the Potomac River at that time.

In 1634 the Marylanders commenced trading with the Massawomeck on the Potomac River. Although they appear in several locations on various maps as late as the Delisle map of ca. 1700, Leonard Calvert's description of the Maryland fur trade in 1634 provides the last contemporary documentary reference to these people. John Lederer provides the last seventeenth-century reference when, in the region beyond the mountains at the headwaters of the Rappahonock River, he notes on his map of 1672, "The Massawomecks dwelt heretofore beyond these mountains."

Thereafter there is silence.

---

[2] It is not certain how much the words for these Iroquoian cheftain names/locations have been altered as a result of Fleet's association with the Potomac River Algonquians and his use of Algonquian interpreters.

[3] On one occasion while trading with the Massawomeck at Great Falls, Fleet met an Indian with "a strange kind of behaviour, using some few words which I learned, but to me it was a foreign language." Later this man returned with a group of *Usserahak* Massawomeck with whom Fleet was able to converse (Neill 1876: 29). Apart from the likelihood of his being Iroquoian, the identity of this foreigner remains unknown.

VII. CONCLUSION

Barring the revelation of heretofore unavailable primary or contemporary documentation regarding the Massawomeck/Antouhonoron, problem-oriented archaeology appears to offer the most realistic opportunity to confirm or deny this hypothesis and to test this model. At present the archaeological data available regarding the period ca. A.D. 1600-1634 for the regions in which the Massawomeck and Antouhonoron are alleged to have resided are not of the nature required to permit the examination of the archaeological reality in this context. Contemporary sites in the Niagara region and in the areas at the headwaters of the Potomac, Monongahela, and Youghiogheny rivers will have to be located and examined in a manner likely to illuminate the problem of Massawomeck/Antouhonoron identity before this archaeological potential can be realized. In the meantime, while awaiting the revelation of additional contemporary documentary evidence or the emergence of cogent archaeological data, this hypothesis is proffered as a plausible explanation of the *evidence* extant.

APPENDIX A

THE LOCATION OF THE ANCHANACHUCK

In his 1608 *True Relation* (Barbour 1969: 186) Smith recounts how late in 1607 Powhatan had told him that the *Anchanachuck* lived ". . . upon the same Sea [with] a mighty Nation called *Pocoughtronack*, a fierce nation that did eat men." This location was confirmed in general terms by the Powell and Todkill account in *The Proceedings* which relates how, during Smith's meeting with the Susquehannock chiefs in the Tockwogh village at the head of Chesapeake Bay in July 1608, the English heard ". . . many descriptions and discourses they made us of *Atquanahucke*, Massawomecke and other people, signifying they inhabit the river of Cannida and from the French have their hatchets and such tooles by trade . . ." (Barbour 1969: 408; Quinn 1979 (5): 323). As a result it was surmised that the location of the *Massawomeck* homeland might become more apparent if the *Anchanachuck* (Atquanahucke, Atquanachukes) homeland were known.

It is noteworthy that when Smith drew the Zúñiga sketch map (Fig. 2), presumably in 1608, he omitted the *Anchanachuck* from this map indicating only the *Pocoughtawonauck* on the inland "sea." This does not appear to be an oversight, for on his 1612 work *Map of Virginia* (Fig. 1), once again he located only the Massawomeck on this hinterland body of water. The omission of the *Atquanahuck* from both these maps appears to reflect information revealed in September 1608 when in a confrontation with Powhatan, Powhatan put Smith right informing him ". . . as for the *Ataquanuchuck* [sic]. . . it is a contrary way from those parts you suppose it" (Barbour 1969: 414). However, there must have been more to this exchange, or some subsequent discussion regarding the location of the Atquanahucke, for in his *General Historie* (1624: 61) Smith appends the following contradictory illuminating comment to the Powell and Todkill account of Smith's meeting with the Susqusahonockes in the Tockwogh village: ". . . but the Atquanachucke are on the Ocean sea."

Smith's *Map of Virginia* reflects this revision to the Powell and Todkill text. He locates the *Atquanachukes* (sic) on the Atlantic Ocean to the north of the head of Chesapeake Bay. However, the location of the crosses shown on this map at the head of Chesapeake Bay, short of the territory Smith attributes to the Atquanachukes, clearly indicates his intelligence ". . . was had by information of the Savages. . ." (Barbour 1969: 344;

Wright and Freund 1953: 50). Thereafter the *Atquanahucke*, in one spelling or another, appear in a location on, or near, Delaware Bay as is evidenced by the Hall map of 1632 (Cumming et al. 1971: 283), the Blaue map of 1635 (ibid.: 293), Barbour's map (1969: 169), and Mooney's account in Hodge's *Handbook* (1907 (1): 112). This location accords well with Tooker's (1894: 183) interpretation of the Algonquian Atquanahucke as meaning "those beyond, or at the end of, the mountains."

As finally and correctly located on the Delaware in the region below present-day New Castle, Delaware, the *Anchanachuck* are remote from the Massawomeck on the "river of Cannida" and the erroneous Powell and Todkill account of the *Anchanachuk* homeland can provide no assistance in the search for the Massawomeck homeland.

APPENDIX B

THE LOCATION OF OCANAHONAN

Accounts of *Ocanahonan* indicating that it was located on or near the "back sea" beyond or in the hinterland mountains are doubly involved in the search for the Massawomeck homeland, Should the Massawomeck and *Ocanahonon* have been neighbors, the successful location of *Ocanahonan* might help locate the Massawomeck homeland. *Ocanahonan*, being the location of Europeans in the hinterland may have served, in some manner, as a source of the European material which the Tockwogh and Susquehannock claimed the Massawomeck to have obtained from the French on the "river of Cannida."

Late in 1607 Powhatan related to Smith that men clothed like him (Smith) lived at a place called *Ocanahonan* on "the course of our river," the James River. In his 1608 *True Relation* Smith indicates that this location was beyond the falls at present-day Richmond, Virginia, but "within four or five daies journey of the falls" where there "was a great turning of *salt* water" (Barbour 1969: 182). It was in this context that Powhatan explained to Smith: "Beyond them [the Massawomeck] he [Powhatan] described [to Smith] people with short Coates, and Sleeves to the Elbowes, that passed that way in Shippes like ours. Many Kingdomes hee described mee the heade of the [Chesapeake] Bay, which seemed to be a mightie River, issuing from mightie Mountains betwixt the two Seas, the people cloathed at Ocamahowan" [sic] (Tyler 1907: 45-46; Barbour 1969: 186).[1]

---

[1] In 1622 Edward Waterhouse (1622: 8-9) described an event experienced by a party of Englishmen who by that date, Waterhouse states, were "planted" at Great Falls. Although not wholly germane in the context of this paper, it is sufficiently reminiscent of accounts purporting Europeans to be west of "Virginia," to warrant inclusion here. " . . . in a voyage made by Lieutenant Marmaduke Parkinson, and other English Gentlemen, up the River of Potomack that saw a China Boxe at one of the Kings houses where they were: Being demanded where he had it, made answer. That it was sent from a King that dwelt in the West, over the great Hills, some tenne dayes iourney whose Countrey is near a great sea, he having that boxe, from a people as he said, that came thither in ships, that weare cloaths, crooked swords, & somewhat like our men, dwelt in houses, and were called Acanack-Chinas and he offered our people, that he would send his Brother along with them to that King, which offer the Governor purposed not to refuse; and the rather, by reason of the continual constant relations of all those Savages in Virginia, of a Sea, and the way to it West, they affirming that the heads of all those seaven goodly Rivers. (the least whereof is greater than the River of Thames, an navigable above an hundred and fifty miles, and not above six or eight miles one from another) which fall all into one great Bay [Chesapeake], have their rising out of a ridge of hills, that runnes all along South

In his *True Relation* Smith also explains that "divers Indians" and "many of the rest not only Opechancanoyes [Powhatan's brother] and an Indian which had beene prisoner to Pehatan [sic] had before tolde mee" confirmed this location for *Ocanahonan* (ibid.).

The location of *Ocanahonan* as expressed in days travel is varied and uncertain because the points of origin are not clear. In Smith's *True Relation* it was within four to five days' journey from the falls at present-day Richmond. Cogently Barbour notes the presence of an ink amendment to a manuscript copy to *True Relation*, which had been inserted before 1630. It reads "as of certaine men at a place 6 dayes iorny beyond *Ocanahonan*" (Barbour 1969: 182, n 2). Smith also notes in his *True Relation* that ". . . some called it five dayes, some sixe, some eight, where the sayde water dashed against many stones and rockes" on the back sea (ibid.: 186). In his *General Historie* (1624: 110) Smith states *Ocanahonan* was "five daies iourney from us," presumably from Jamestown. Significantly the accounts of three voyages to the falls at Richmond, made by Captain Newport, Gabriel Archer, and two unknown voyagers in search of the source of the James River, make no mention of *Ocanahonan* (Barbour 1969: 80-98, 102) which allegedly lay the various distances noted above beyond Richmond.

In his *Historie* William Strachey mentions *Ochanahoen* (sic) in a wholly different context. In his description of the people who live beyond the hinterland mountains Strachey states: ". . . to the Southward where at *Peccarecanick* [*Pakerakanick* on the Zúñiga map of 1608] and *Ochanahoen* by the relation of *Machumps* [a Powhatan Indian who had been to England] the people have houses build of stone walls, and one storey above another so taught them by the English who escaped the slaughter at Roanoke." (Wright and Freund 1953: 34). A note on the Zúñiga map states that four Roanoke survivors lived at this *Pakerakanick* location (Barbour 1969: 240, 264).

The instructions provided for Sir Thomas Gates in anticipation of his becoming governor at Jamestown also mentions *Ocanahonan* in a context which place it south of Jamestown. Confused as Gates's instructions are at times, they clearly state: "Four dayes Journey from your forte [Jamestown] Southward is a town called *Ohonahorn* [sic] seated where the River of Choanoke [Chowan] divideth it self into three branches and falleth into the sea of Rawnoke [Albemarle Sound]" (Barbour 1969: 264).

This location is alleged to be some twenty miles from *Caththega* (sic). Barbour (ibid.: 182, 264) notes that the amended *True Relation* manuscript in the British Museum also corrects the spelling of *Ohohahorn* in the

---

and North: whereby they doubt not but to find a safe, easie, and good passage to the South Sea, part by water, and part by land, esteeming it not above an hundred and fifty miles from the head of the Falls [Great Falls], where we are now planted, the Discovery whereof will bring forth a most rich trade to Cathay, China, Iapan, and those other of the East Indies, to the inestimable benefit of this Kingdome."

manuscript to read "*onahawan*" and suggests that *Caththega* may be the *Cataking* shown on the Chowan River on the Velasco map of 1610 or 1611 (Cumming et al. 1971; 266-67; Quinn 1979 (5): fig. 140).

If *Ocanahonan* was south of Jamestown, the possibility arises that it may be Lane's *Oanoke*, or *Ohanoke*, the Choanoke village visited by Lane from the Roanoke settlement in the spring of 1586 (Quinn 1955 (1): 259; 1979 (3): 296). There Lane heard how a powerful chief to the north, which was probably Powhatan, had ". . . traffike with white men who have clothes as we have." It seems likely that Lane's remarks refer to trade late in the sixteenth century between Powhatan and the Europeans who had frequented Chesapeake Bay before 1586, the ill-fated Jesuit mission at Axacan in 1570 being but one example. Nevertheless as Barbour has noted (1969: 240), neither *Oconohowan*, in any of its various spellings, or *Pakerakanick* are mentioned in the accounts of the Roanoke colony.

These confusing accounts, and the speculation they have generated regarding *Ocanahouan*, appear to be laid to rest by a tangential remark made in 1611 by Sir Thomas Dale, then Marshall of Virginia: ". . . this summer Cole and Kitchins plot with three more [deserters] binding their course to *Ocanohowan* five daies journey from us [where] they report the Spanish inhabiting" (Arber 1884: 508). This places *Ocanahowan* on the Atlantic coast five days journey south of Chesapeake Bay in a region where the Spanish were active, remote from the homeland of the Massawomeck located by Smith on a hinterland sea in the Chesapeake Bay latitudes. However, modern scholars are not all agreed on the location proposed by Sir Thomas. Quinn (1973: 459; 1985: 371) has suggested that the Europeans at *Ocamahowan* (sic) may be either the French on the St. Lawrence River or a village on the Roanoke River.

REFERENCES

Anomymous 1972
  An Historical Account of the Doings and The Sufferings of the Chris-
  tian Indians in New England in the years 1675, 1676, 1677 . . . etc.
  Reprinted in 1836 in *Archaeologica American. Transactions and Collec-
  tions of the American Antiquarian Society*, Vol. 2. Cambridge. Re-
  printed in 1972 in the series, *Research Library of Colonial America*. Arno
  Press. New York.
Abbott, William W. 1967
  A Virginia Chronology 1585-1783. *Virginia 350th Anniversary Celebration
  Corporation, Historical Booklet Number 2*. Garrett and Massie Inc. Rich-
  mond, Virginia.
Abler, Thomas S. and Elisabeth Tooker 1978
  Seneca. *Handbook of North American Indians*. Volume 15, Northeast.
  Bruce G. Trigger ed. Smithsonian Institution.
Arber Edward, ed. 1884
  *Capt. John Smith President of Virginia and Admiral of New England. Works
  1608-1631*. The English Scholars Library No. 16. Birmingham. *Capt.
  John Smith of Willougyby Alford, Lincolnshire; President of Virginia and
  Admiral of New England. Works. 1608-1631*. The English Scholars Li-
  brary of Old and Modern Works. 2 parts, Edward Arber ed. West-
  minister. Reprinted Edinburgh, 1910 (2 vols.) with introduction by
  A.G. Bailey. Reprinted *Travels and Works of Captain John Smith Pres-
  ident of Virginia and Admiral of New England 1580-1631*, Burt Franklin
  Research and Source Works Series No. 130, 2 vols. (American Clas-
  sics in History and Social Science No. 15). Burt Franklin, New York.
Archer, Gabriel 1607
  A relatyon of the Discovery of our River, from James Forte into the
  Maine. In *The Jamestown Voyages Under the First Charter 1606-1609*,
  Philip L. Barbour ed., pp. 80-98. (See Philip L. Barbour).
Asher, George Michael 1963
  Henry Hudson, The Navigator. Burt Franklin Reprint Co.
Bancroft, George 1844
  History of the United States from the Discovery of the American Continent.
  3 volumes. Charles C. Little and James Brown. Boston.
Barbour, Philip L.
  1964
    The Three Worlds of Captain John Smith. Houghton, Mifflin Company,
    Riverside Press, Cambridge, Boston.

1969

   The Jamestown Voyages Under the First Charter. Hakluyt Society, 2
   volumes, Series 2, Volume CXXXVI. Cambridge University Press.
   London.

1986

   The Complete Works of Captain John Smith (1580-1631), 3 vols. Institute
   of Early American History and Culture. Williamsburg, Virginia.
   University of North Carolina. Chapel Hill.

Beauchamp, William M.

   1889 (a)

   The Origin and Early Life of the New York Iroquois. *Transactions
   Oneida Historical Society*, 1887-89. Oneida, New York. Paper delivered to the Oneida Historical Society, March 20th, 1886.

   1889 (b)

   Cayuga Indian Relics, *American Naturalist*, Vol. 23. Salem.

   1892

   Early Religions of the Iroquois. *The American Antiquarian and Oriental
   Journal*, Vol. 14.

   1894

   The Origin of the Iroquois. *The American Antiquarian and Oriental
   Journal*, Vol. 16, No. 2.

   1895

   Indian Nations of the Great Lakes. *American Antiquarian* Vol. 17.

   1898

   Earthenware of the New York Aborigines. Bulletin of the New York State
   Museum, Vol. 5, No. 22. Albany.

   1905

   A History of the New York Iroquois. New York State Museum, Bull.
   No. 78.

Biggar, Henry P.

   1922-1936

   The Works of Samuel de Champlain. 6 vols. Champlain Society. Toronto.

   1924

   Voyages of Jacques Cartier. Public Archives, Ottawa. Publication No.
   11.

Bishop, Morris 1948

   Champlain, The Life of Fortitude. Alfred A. Knopf, New York.

Bozman, John Leeds 1837

   *The History of Maryland, from its First Settlement in 1633 to the Restoration
   in 1660*. James Lucas & E.K. Deaver. Baltimore.

Bradley, James W.

   1979

   The Onondaga Iroquois: 1550-1655, A Study in Acculturative
   Change and its Consequences. Unpublished Ph.D. dissertation,
   Syracuse University. Syracuse, New York.

1987
  Evolution of the Onondaga Iroquois: Accommodating Change 1500-1655.
  Syracuse University Press. Syracuse, New York.
Brashler, Janet G. 1987
  A Middle 16th Century Susquehannock Village in Hampshire County,
  West Virginia. *West Virginia Archaeologist*, Vol. 39: (2).
Brasser, T. J. 1978
  Early Indian-European Contacts. *Handbook of North American Indians*,
  Volume 15:78–88, Northeast, Bruce G. Trigger ed. Smithsonian In-
  stitution.
Brinton, D.G. 1884
  *The Lenape and their Legends with a complete text of Walam Olam a New
  Translation and an Enquiry into its Authenticity.* Philadelphia. AMS
  Reprint 1969. New York.
Brown, Alexander 1890
  *The Genesis of the United States. A Narrative of the Movement in England,
  1605-1616, which resulted in the Plantation of North America by English-
  men.* 2 vols. Boston. Reprinted 1964 by Russel and Russell. New
  York.
Bushnell, David I. Jr.
  1907
    Virginia-From the Early Records. *American Anthropologist*, New Se-
    ries, Vol. 9, No. 1.
  1908
    Research in Virginia from Tidewater to the Alleghenies. *American
    Anthropologist*, Vol. 10, No. 4.
  1930
    The Five Monacan Towns in Virginia, 1607. *Smithsonian Miscella-
    neous Collection*, Vol. 82, No. 12. Washington.
  1935
    The Manahoac Tribes in Virginia, 1608. *Smithsonian Miscellaneous
    Collection*, Vol. 94, No. 8. Washington.
  1937
    Indian Sites below the Falls of the Rappahannock, Virginia. *Smith-
    sonian Miscellaneous Collection*, Vol. 96, No. 4. Washington.
  1940
    Virginia before Jamestown. *Smithsonian Miscellaneous Collection*, Vol.
    100. Washington.
Cadzow, Donald A. 1936
  Safe Harbor Report No. 2. Archaeological Section. Pennsylvania Historical
  and Museum Commission. Harrisburg.
Campisi, Jack 1978
  Oneida. *Handbook of North American Indians*, Volume 15:481–90, North-
  east, Bruce G. Trigger ed. Smithsonian Institution.
Ceci, Lynn 1977
  The Effect of European Contact and Trade on the Settlement Pattern

of Indians in Coastal New York 1524-1655. Unpublished Ph.D. dissertation. City University of New York Graduate Center.

Chafe, Wallace L. 1967
Seneca Morphology and Dictionary. *Smithsonian Contributions to Anthropology*, No. 4. Washington.

Clinton, De Witt 1820
Memoir of the Antiquities of the Western Part of the State of New York. Paper read before Literacy and Philosophical Society of New York, October 7th, 1817. Second printing E. & E. Hosford, Albany. Reprinted 1916 by W. Abbott, Tarrytown, New York.

Cumming, William P. 1982
Early Maps of the Chesapeake Bay Area: Their Relation to Settlement and Society. In *Early Maryland in a Wider World*: 267–310, David B. Quinn ed. Wayne State University Press. Detroit.

Cumming, William. P. and Douglas L. Right 1958
The Discoveries of John Lederer with unpublished letters by and about Lederer to Governor John Winthrop Jr. and an essay on the Indians of the Lederer Discoveries. University of Virginia Press, Charlottesville, Virginia. Wochovia Historical Society. Winston-Salem. North Carolina.

Cumming, William. P., R.A. Skelton and David B. Quinn 1971
The Discovery of North America. McClelland & Stewart, Toronto.

Dunbar, Helen R. and Katherine C. Ruhl 1974
Copper Artifacts from the Engelbert Site. *New York State Archaeological Association*, Bulletin 61-1:1–10.

Fausz, J. Frederick 1985
Forgotton Men with Fruitful Dreams: The Significance of the Chesapeake Bay Beaver Trade, 1580-1660. Paper read at the Fifth North American Fur Trade Conference. McGill University, Montreal.

Feest, Christian F.
1978
Nanticoke and Neighboring Tribes. *Handbook of North American Indians*, Volume 15:240–52. Northeast. Bruce G. Trigger ed. Smithsonian Institution.
1978 (a)
Virginia Algonquians. *Handbook of North American Indians*, Volume 15:253–70. Northeast. Bruce G. Trigger ed. Smithsonian Institution.
1978 (b)
North Carolina Algonquians. *Handbook of North American Indians*, Volume 15:271–81. Northeast. Bruce G. Trigger editor. Smithsonian Institution.

Feister, Lois M. 1978
Linguistic Communications between the Dutch and Indians in New Netherland, 1609-1664. In "Neighbors and Intruders: An Ethnohistorical Exploration of the Indians of Hudson's River." Lawrence M. Hauptman and Jack Campisi eds. *National Museum of Man Mer-*

cury Series, Canadian Ethnology Service, Paper No. 39:181–96. National Museums of Canada, Ottawa.

Fenton, William N. 1940
Problems Arising from the Historic Northeastern Position of the Iroquois. *Smithsonian Miscellaneous Collection*, Volume 100.

Fitzgerald, William R. 1982
Lest the Beaver Run Loose: The early 17th Century Christianson Site and Trends in Historic Neutral Archaeology. *National Museum of Man Mercury Series*, Archaeological Survey of Canada Paper No. 111. National Museums of Canada. Ottawa.

Fowke, Gerard 1894
Archaeological Investigations in the James and Potomac Valleys. *Bureau of American Ethnology*, Bulletin No. 23. Washington.

Gallatin, Albert 1836
A Synopsis of the Indian Tribes within the United States east of the Rocky Mountains and in the British and Russian Possessions in North America. 3 volumes. *Transactions and Collections, American Antiquities Society*, No. 22. Worcester, Massachusetts.

Gatschet, Albert S. 1881
The Massawomeckes. *The American Antiquarian and Oriental Journal*, Volume 3, No. 4.

Gendron, F. 1868
Quelques particularitez de pays des Hurons en la nouvelle France, remarquées par le Sieure Gendron, docteur en médecine qui a demeuré dans ce pays-là fort lotemps. *Shea's Cramoisy Press Series*, No. 25. J. Munsell. Albany.

Goddard, Ives
1978
Mascouten. *Handbook of North American Indians*, Volume 15:668–72, Northeast. Bruce G. Trigger ed. Smithsonian Institution.
1978 (a)
Delaware. *Handbook of North American Indians*, Volume 15:213–39, Northeast. Bruce G. Trigger ed. Smithsonian Institution.

Gookin, Daniel 1792
Historical Collections of the Indians in New England (1674). In Massachusetts Historical Society, *Collections* 1st Serial, I. Boston.

Gookin, Daniel 1792
Historical Collections of the Indians in New England (1674). In Massachusetts Historical Society, *Collections* 1st Serial, I. Boston.

Goss, John 1990a
Blaeu's 'The Great Atlas' of the 17th Century World. Studio Editions in Cooperation with the Royal Geographical Society. London.
1990b
The Mapping of North America: Three Centuries of Map-making 1500–1860. The Wellfleet Press, New Jersey for Studio Editions Ltd. London.

Griffin, James B. 1978
 Late Prehistory of the Ohio Valley. *Handbook of North American Indians*, Volume 15:547–59. Northeast. Bruce G. Trigger ed. Smithsonian Institution.

Hamelin, Jean 1966
 Bourdon, Jean. *Dictionary of Canadian Biography*, Volume 1. George W. Brown, general ed. University of Toronto Press, Toronto.

Hanna, Charles A. 1911
 The Wilderness Trail: or, the Ventures and Adventures of the Pennsylvania Traders on the Allegheny Path with Some New Annals of the Old West, and the Records of Some Strong Men and Some Bad Ones. 2 vols. New York and London. G.P. Putnam's sons. Reprinted Ann Arbor 1967.

Hawley, Charles
 1879
  Early Chapters of Cayuga History: Jesuit Missions in Cio-o-Gouen 1656-1684. Also an Account of the Sulpitian Mission Among the Cayugas, About Quinte Bay, in 1668. Knapp & Peck. Auburn N.Y.
 1884
  Early Chapters of Seneca History: Jesuit Missions in Sonnontouan 1656-1684. Cayuga County Historical Collection, No. 3. Auburn, New York.

Heidenreich, Conrad
 1971
  Huronia: A History and Geography of the Huron Indians 1600-1650. McClelland & Stewart Ltd. Toronto.
 1976
  Explorations and Mapping of Samuel de Champlain, 1603-1632. Cartographica, Monograph No. 17, being Supplement No. 2 to *Canadian Cartographer*, Vol. 13, 1976, Monograph No. 17, James R. Gibson editor. University of Toronto Press. Toronto.
 1988
  An Analysis of the 17th Century Mape 'Nouvelle France'. *Cartographica* Vol. 25, No.3: 67-111.

Heisey, Henry W. and J. Paul Witner 1962
 Of Historic Susquehannock Cemeteries. *Pennsylvania Archaeologist* Vol. 32, Nos 3-4:99–130.

Hewitt, J.N.B. 1910
 Susquehanna. *Handbook of American Indians North of Mexico*, Frederick W. Hodge editor. Bureau of American Ethnology, Bulletin 30, Part 2. Smithsonian Institution.

Hodge, Frederick Webb (editor) 1907-1910
 Handbook of American Indians North of Mexico. Bureau of American Ethnology, Bulletin 30, Parts 1 and 2.

Hoffman, Bernard G.
 1964
  Observations on Certain Ancient Tribes of the Northern Appala-

chian Province. Anthropological Paper No. 70. *Smithsonian Insti-tution Bureau of Ethnology*, Bulletin 191.

1967

Ancient Tribes Revisted: A Summary of Indian Distribution and Movement in the Northeastern United States from 1534 to 1779. *Ethnohistory* Vol. 14, 1-2.

Hunt, George T. 1940

The Wars of the Iroquois: A Study in Intertribal Trade Relations. University of Wisconsin Press. Madison.

Hunter, William A.

1959

The Historic Role of the Susquehannock. In *Susquehannock Miscellany*, 8–18, John Witthoft and W. Fred Kinsey editors. The Pennsylvania Historical and Museum Commission. Harrisburg, Pennsylvania.

1978

History of the Ohio Valley. *Handbook of North American Indians*, Volume 15, Northeast: 588–93. Bruce G. Trigger ed. Smithsonian Institution.

Jameson, J. Franklin 1909

Narratives of New Netherland, 1609-1664. Charles Scribner's Sons. Reprinted by Barnes and Noble, New York, 1959.

Jefferson, Thomas 1904

Notes on the State of Virginia, 1781-82. Reprinted in *The Works of Thomas Jefferson*, 1892-1899, 12 volumes. Paul Leicester Ford editor. Federal Edition. Philadelphia.

Jennings, Francis

1968

Glory, Death, and Transfiguration: the Susquehannock Indians of the Seventeenth Century. *Proceedings of the American Philosophical Society*. Vol. 112.

1978

Susquehannock. *Handbook of North American Indians*. Volume 15:362–67, Northeast. Bruce G. Trigger ed. Smithsonian Institution.

1982

Indians and Frontiers in Seventeenth-Century Maryland. In *Early Maryland in a Wider World*:216–41, David B. Quinn ed. Wayne State University Press. Detroit.

Johnson, Adrian 1974

America Explored: A Cartographic History of the Exploration of North America. Viking Press. New York.

Kent, Barry C. 1984

Susquehanna's Indians. Anthropology Series Number 6, Commonwealth of Pennsylvania. The Pennsylvania Historical and Museum Commission. Harrisburg.

Kent, Bretton W. 1982
An Overlooked Busycon Whelk (Melongenidae) from the Eastern United Sates. *The Nautilus* Volume 93 (3).

Kinsey, W. Fred III 1969
Historic Susquehannock Pottery. In *Susquehannock Miscellany*:61–98. J. Witthoft and W. Fred Kinsey III editors. The Pennsylvania Historical and Museum Commission. Harrisburg.

Lankford, John 1967
Captain John Smith's America: Selections from his writings. Harper Torchbooks. Harper & Row. New York, Evanston & London.

Laverdière, Charles Honore 1870
Oeuvre de Champlain. Imprimé au Séminaire par George E. Desbarats. Quebec.

Le Blant, R. and R. Beaudry 1967
Nouveaux documents sur Champlain et son époque. Volume 1 (1560-1622). Public Archives of Canada, Publication No. 15. Ottawa.

Lounsbury, Floyd G. 1960
Iroquois Place-names in the Champlain Valley. Reprinted by the University of the State of New York, State Education Department. Albany.

Lucy, Charles L. and Richard J. McCracken 1985
Blackman Site (36BR83): A Proto-Susquehannock Village. *Pennsylvania Archaeologist*, Volume 55 (1-2):5–29.

Lupold, Harry Forrest 1975
The Forgotten People: The Woodland Erie. Exposition Press. Hicksville, New York.

Margry, Pierre 1876-1886
Découvertes et établissements des François dans l'ouest et dans le sud de l'Amérique septentionale, 1614-1754. Mémoires et documents originaux. 5 vols. D. Jouaust ed. Paris.

Marshall, Orasmus H. 1887
The Historical Writings of the Late Orasmus H. Marshall Relating to the History of the West with an Introduction by William L. Stone. Joel Munsell's Sons. Albany.

McCary, Ben C. 1857
Indians in Seventeenth Century Virginia. Virginia 350th Anniversary Celebration Corporation, Historical Booklet No. 18. Williamsburg, Virginia.

McCary, Ben C. and Norman F. Barka 1977
John Smith and the Zúñiga Maps in the Light of Recent Archaeological Investigations along the Chickahominy River. *Archaeology of Eastern North America*, Volume 5.

McCracken, Richard J. 1985
Susquehannocks, Brule and Carantouannais: A Continuing Research Problem. *The Bulletin and Journal of Archaeology for New York State*, No. 91. New York State Archaeological Assoc.

Menard, Russel R. and Lois Green Carr 1982
  The Lords Baltimore and the Colonization of Maryland. In *Early Maryland in a Wider World*:167–215, David B. Quinn ed. Wayne State University Press. Detroit.
Merrill, James H. 1979
  Cultural Continuity among the Piscataway Indians of Colonial Maryland. *William and Mary Quarterly*, 3rd Series, Volume 36, No. 4.
Miner, Charles 1845
  History of Wyoming in a series of letters from Charles Miner to his son William Penn Miner. J. Crissy. Philadelphia.
Moir, John S. 1966
  Sir David Kirke. *Dictionary of Canadian Biography*, Vol. 1, 1000 to 1700. University of Toronto.
Mook, Maurice A.
  1943
    The Anthropological Position of the Indian Tribes of Tidewater Virginia. *William and Mary Quarterly*, 2nd Series, Vol. 23, No. 1.
  1943 (a)
    Virginia Ethnology from an Early Relation. *William and Mary Quarterly*, 2nd Series, vol. 23, No. 2
  1943 (b)
    The Ethnological Significance of Tindall's Map of Virginia, 1608. *William and Mary Quarterly*, 2nd Series, Vol. 23, No. 4
Mooney, James
  1889
    Indian Tribes of the District of Columbia, *American Anthropologist*, Old Series, Vol. 2.
  1895
    The Siouan Tribes of the East. *Bureau of American Ethnology*, Bulletin No. 22. Washington.
  1907
    The Powhatan Confederacy Past and Present. *American Anthropologist*, New Series, Vol. 9, No. 1.
  1907 (a)
    Accohanoc. In *Handbook of American Indians North of Mexico*. Bureau of American Ethnology, Bulletin No. 30, Part 1.
  1907 (b)
    Accomac. In *Handbook of American Indians North of Mexico*. Bureau of American Ethnology, Bulletin No. 30, Part 1.
  1910
    Powhatan Confederacy. In *Handbook of American Indians North of Mexico*. Bureau of American Ethnology, Bulletin No. 30.
Morrison, A.J. 1921
  The Virginia Indian Trade to 1673. *William and Mary Quarterly* History Magazine, 2nd Series, Volume 1, No. 4.

Mouer, Daniel L. 1983
A Review of the Archaeology and the Ethnology of the Monacans. In *Piedmont Archaeology*. J. Mark Wittkofski and Lyle E. Browning editors. Archaeological Society of Virginia, Special Publication No. 10A.

Murray, Louise Welles 1908
A History of Old Tioga Point and Early Athens, Pennsylvania. Athens, Pennsylvania.

Neill, Edward D. 1876
A Brief Journal of a Voyage made in the Bark Virginia to Virginia and Other Parts of the Continent of America. In *The Founders of Maryland as Portrayed in Manuscripts, Provincial Records and Early Documents*. Joell Munsell. Albany.

Niemczycki, Mary Ann Palmer 1984
The Origin and Development of the Seneca and Cayuga Tribes of New York State. Research Records No. 17. Rochester Museum and Science Center. Rochester.

Noble, William C. 1980
The Protohistoric Revisited. Unpublished paper presented at Canadian Archaeological Association Annual Meeting. Saskatoon, Saskatchewan.

Parkman, Francis
1865
Pioneers of France in the New World. 1909 Little. Brown, and Company edition, Boston.
1899
The Jesuits in North America in the Seventeenth Century. George N. Morang and Company edition, Toronto.

Peden, William 1955
Thomas Jefferson's Notes on the State of Virginia. University of North Carolina Press, Chapel Hill.

Pendergast, James F.
1985
Were the French of Lake Ontario in the Sixteenth Century? *Man in the Northeast*, No. 29:71–85. Albany, New York.
1989
The Significance of Some Marine Shell on Ontario Iroquois Archaeological Sites. *Proceedings of the 1986 Shell Bead Conference: Selected Papers*: 97–112. Research Records No. 20 Rochester Museum and Science Center. Rochester, N.Y. Charles F. Hayes III General editor.

Percy, George 1613
Observations gathered out of a Discourse of the Plantation of the Southern Colonie in Virginia by the English, 1606. In *The Jamestown Voyages under the First Charter 1606-1609*, Philip P. Barbour ed. (See Philip L. Barbour.)

Portinaro, Pierluigi and Franco Knirsch 1987
The Cartography of North America: 1500-1800. Facts on File, Inc. A Bison Book

Pratt, Peter P. 1976
Archaeology of the Oneida Iroquois, Vol. 1. Occasional Publications in Northeastern Anthropology No. 1. Man in Northeast. Minot Printing and Binding. Greenfield, MA.

Purchas, Samuel 1625
Hakluytus Posthumus or Purchas-his Pilgrimes. 20 vols. James MacLehose and Doves. 1905. Glasgow.

Quinn, David B.
1955
The Roanoke Voyages, 2 vols. Hakluyt Society, Second Series, Nos. 104, 105. London.

1973
England and the Discovery of America 1481-1620. Alfred A. Knopf. New York.

1974
The Hakluyt Handbook. 2 vols. D.B. Quinn editor. Hakluyt Society, Second Series, No. 145.

1977
North America From Earliest Discovery to First Settlement: The Norse Voyages to 1612. Harper Row Publishers. New York, Hagerstown, San Francisco, London.

1979
New American World: A Documentary History of North America to 1612. 5 vols. Arno Press, New York.

1985
Set Fair for Roanoke: Voyages and Colonies. 1584-1606. University of Carolina Press. Chapel Hill and London.

Royce, C.C. 1881
An Enquiry into the Identity of the History of the Shawnee Indians. *American Antiquarian,* Vol. 3, No. 3.

Sagard, Gabriel 1636
Histoire au Canada et voyages que les frères mineurs Recollects y ont faicts pour la conversion des infidelles depuis l'an 1615 . . . avec une dictionnaire de la langue Huronne. Troisième Parti. 2 vols. Claude Sonnuis, Paris. Reprinted in 4 vols., 1866. E. Tross Paris.

Scarf, J. Thomas 1879
History of Maryland from the Earliest Period to the Present Day. Facsimile edition published by Tradition Press. Hatboro, Pennsylvania.

Schaeffer, Claude E. 1942
The Tutelo Indians in Pennsylvania History. Introduction to *The Tutelo Adoption Ceremony.* Frank G. Speck ed. Pennsylvania Historical Commission. Harrisburg.

Schoolcraft, Henry R.
  1847
    Notes on the Iroquois or Contributions to American History, Antiquities and General Ethnology. Erasmus H. Pease & Co., Albany. 1846 edition published by Bartlett and Welford, New York.
  1855
    Information Respecting the History, Condition and Prospects of the Indian Tribes of the United States collected and prepared under the direction of the Bureau of Indian Affairs per act of Congress, March 3rd, 1847. Lippincott & Company. Philadelphia.
  1857
    History of the Indian Tribes of the United States, their Present Condition and Prospects and Sketch of their Ancient Status. Part 6. J.P. Lippincott & Co. Philadelphia.
Shea, John Gilmary
  1870
    History and General Description of New France by Rev. P.F.X. de Charlevois, S.J. 6 vols. Reprinted by Loyola University Press 1962.
  1878
    Champlain's Expedition into Western New York in 1615 and the Recent Identification of the Fort by General John S. Clark. *The Pennsylvania Magazine of History and Biography*, Volume 2. Historical Society of Pennsylvania, Philadelphia.
  1884
    The Jesuits, Recollects and the Indians. In *Narrative and Critical History of America*, Justine Winsor ed. Vol. 4. French Explorations and Settlement in North America and those of the Portuguese, Dutch and Swedes. Houghton, Mifflin and Company. Boston and New York.
Smith, John
  1608
    A True Relation of Such Occurrences and Accidents of Noate as hath hapned in Virginia since the first planting of the Colony. (See Barbour 1969.)
  1612
    A Map of Virginia with a Description of the Covntrey, the Commodities, People, Government and Religion. (See Barbour 1969.)
  1612
    The Proceedings of the English Colonie in Virginia since their first beginning from England in the years of our Lord 1606, till this present 1612, with all their accidents that befell them in their Iournies and Discoveries. Title for the second part of Smith's Map of Virginia. (See Barbour 1969.)
  1624
    The General Historie of Virginia, New England and the Summer Isles with the names of Adventurers, Planters and Governours from the beginings An: 1584 to this present 1624. London. Facsimile edition University

Microfilms Inc. 1966. Ann Arbor. March of America Facsimile Series, Number 18.

Snow, Dean R. 1978
Eastern Abenaki. *Handbook of North American Indians*, Volume 15:137–47, Northeast, Bruce G. Trigger ed. Smithsonian Institution.

Speck, Frank G.
1907
Some Outlines of Aboriginal Culture in the Southeastern United States. *American Anthropologist*, New Series, Vol. 9, No. 2.
1924
The Ethnic Position of the Southeastern Algonquian. *American Anthopologist*, New Series, Vol. 26, No. 2.
1927
The Nanticoke and Conoy Indians. *Papers of the Historical Society of Delaware*, New Series 1. Wilmington.
1928
Chapters on the Ethnology of the Powhatan Tribes of Virginia. In *Indian Notes and Monographs*, Vol. 1, No. 5. F.W. Hodge ed. Museum of American Indian. Heye Foundation. New York.

Spelman, Henry 1910
Relation of Virginea, 1609. In *Travels and Works of Captain John Smith, President of Virginia and Admiral of New England*. 2 vols. Edward Arber ed. introduction by A.G. Bailey. Burt Franklin: Research and Source Works Series, No. 130; American Classics in History and Social Science, No. 15. Burt Franklin. New York.

Steckley, John
1985
Why did the Wenro Turn Turtle? *Arch Notes* 85/3, Newsletter of the Ontario Archaeology Society. Toronto.
1985 a
A Tale of Two Peoples. *Arch. Notes* 85(4): 9–15. Newsletter of the Ontario Archaeological Society. Toronto.

Stewart, T.D.
1928
Chapters on the Ethnology of the Powhatan Tribes of Virginia. *Indian Notes and Monographs*, F.W. Hodge ed. Museum of American Indian, Heye Foundation, Vol. 1, No. 5.
1939
Excavating the Indian Village of Patawomeke (Potomac). *Explorations and Field Work of the Smithsonian Institution in 1938*. Washington.

Stith, William 1747
The History of the First Discovery and Settlement of Virginia. Williamsburg. Reprinted 1969, Daniel B. Rutman ed. Johnson Reprint Company. New York and London.

Strachey, William 1953
The Historie of Travell into Virginia Britania (1612). Louis B. Wright and
Virginia Freund eds. Hakluyt Society, Second Series Vol. 103. Lon-
don.
Swanton, John R.
1928
Aboriginal Cultures of the Southeast. *Bureau of American Ethnology*,
Bulletin No. 42. Smithsonian Institution.
1935
Notes on the Cultural Province of the Southeast. *American Anthro-
pologist*, New Series Vol. 37, No. 3.
1946
Indians of the Southeastern United States. *Bureau of American Eth-
nology*, Bulletin No. 137. Smithsonian Institution.
1952
The Indian Tribes of North America. *Bureau of American Ethnology*
Bulletin 145. Smithsonian Institution.
Talbot, Sir William 1672
*The Discoveries of John Lederer in three Marches from Virginia to the West
of Carolina and other parts of the Continent Begun March 1669 and ended
in September 1670.* London 1672. (See Cumming and Right 1958.)
Thomson, Charles 1904
Appendix in *The Works of Thomas Jefferson*, 12 vols. Paul Leicester Ford
ed. G.P. Putnam's Sons. New York and London.
Thwaites, R.G. 1895-1901
*The Jesuit Relations and Allied Documents. Travels and Explorations of the
Jesuit Missionaries in New France. 1610-1791.* 73 vols. Cleveland.
Tooker, William Wallace
1894
The Algonquian Terms Potawomeke and Massawomeke. *American
Anthropologist*, Vol. 7, No. 2. Reprinted 1964 by Kraus Reprint
Corporation, New York.
1901
The Bocootawanaukes; of The Fire Nation. *The Algonquian Series*,
No. 6. New York.
Trigger, Bruce G.
1976
The Children of Aataentsic: A History of the Huron People to 1660 2 vols.
McGill-Queens University Press. Montreal and London.
1978
Handbook of North American Indians, William C. Sturtevant, general
editor Volume 15, Northeast. Bruce G. Trigger, volume ed. Smith-
sonian Institution. Washington.
1985
Natives and Newcomers: Canada's "Heroic Age" Reconsidered. McGill-
Queens University Press. Kingston and Montreal.

1988
   Review of *Evolution of the Onondaga Iroquois: Accommodating Change,
   1500-1655* by James W. Bradley 1987. University of Syracuse Press.
   In *The Canadian Historical Review*. Volume 69, No. 2:257–58.
Tuck, James A. 1971
   Onondaga Iroquois Prehistory: A Study in Settlement Archaeology. Syracuse
   University Press. Syracuse. New York.
Tyler, Lyon Gardiner
1893
   Editorial comment on the Jamestown colony. *William and Mary Quar-
   terly*, Volume 2, No. 1.
1901
   Editorial comment on the Jamestown colony. *William and Mary Quar-
   terly*, Volume 4, No. 1; Volume 9, No. 4.
1907
   Narrative of Early Virginia: 1606-1625. Original Narratives of Early
   American History, Vol. 5. Barnes & Noble. New York, Scribner's
   Sons, New York.
Washburn, Wilcombe E. 1978
   Seventeenth-Century Indian Wars. *Handbook of North American Indians*,
   Volume 15:89–100. Northeast. Bruce G. Trigger ed. Smithsonian
   Institution.
Waterhouse, Edward 1622
   Declaration of the State of the Colony and Affaires in Virginia (etc.) G. Eld
   for Robert Mybourne. London. Reprinted in 1970 as Number 276
   in the series *The English Experience. Its Record in Early Printed Books
   Published in Facsimile*. De Capo Press, Theatrum Orbis Terrarum Ltd.
   Amsterdam, New York.
Weslager, Clinton A.
1942
   Indian Tribes of the Delmarva Peninsula. *Archaeological Society of
   Delaware*, Vol. 3, No. 5.
1972
   The Delaware Indians: A History. Rutgers University Press. New Bruns-
   wick, New Jersey.
1983
   The Nanticoke Indians: Past and Present, University of Delaware Press.
   Newark.
Wise, Jennings Cropper 1911
   *Ye Kingdome of Accawacke, on the Eastern Shore of Virginia in the Seven-
   teenth Century*. Bell Book and Stationery Company. Richmond.
White, Marian E.
1961
   Iroquois Culture History in the Niagara Frontier Area of New York State.
   Museum of Anthropology, University of Michigan, Anthropol-
   ogy. Paper No. 16. Ann Arbor.

1971

Ethnic Identification and Iroquois Groups in Western New York and Ontario. *Ethnohistory*, Vol. 18, No. 1.

1972

On Delineating the Neutral Iroquois of the Eastern Niagara Peninsula of Ontario. *Ontario Archaeology* No. 17:62–74. Ontario Archaeological Society. Toronto.

1978

Neutral and Wenro. *Handbook of North American Indians*, Volume 15:407–11. Northeast. Bruce G. Trigger ed. Smithsonian Institution.

1978 (a)

Erie. *Handbook of North American Indians*. Volume 15:412–17, Northeast. Bruce G. Trigger ed. Smithsonian Institution.

White, Marian E., William E. Engelbrecht and Elisabeth Tooker 1978

Cayuga. *Handbook of North American Indians*. Volume 15:500–04, Northeast. Bruce G. Trigger ed. Smithsonian Institution.

Willoughby, Charles C. 1907

The Virginia Indians in the Seventeenth Century. *American Anthropologist*, Vol. 9, No. 1.

Witthoft, John 1959

Ancestry of the Susquehannock. In *Susquehannock Miscellany*:19–59. John Witthoft and W. Fred Kinsey III eds. The Pennsylvania Historical and Museum Commission. Harrisburg, Pennsylvania.

Witthoft, John 1969

Ancestry of the Susquehannocks. In *Susquehannock Miscellany* 19–98, J. Witthoft and W. Fred Kinsey III editors. The Pennsylvania Historical and Museum Commision. Harrisburg.

Wray, Charles F. 1973

Manual for Seneca Iroquois Archaeology. Cultures Primitive. Honeoye Falls, N.Y.

Wray, Charles F., Martha L. Sempowski, Lorraine P. Saunders, Gian Carlo Cervone 1987

The Adams and Cuthbertson Sites. Charles F. Wray Series in Seneca Archaeology, Vol. 1. Research Records No. 19. Charles F. Hayes III ed. Rochester Museum and Science Center. Rochester.

Wright, Louis B. and Virginia Freund, eds. 1953

The Historie of Travell into Virginia Britania, by William Strachey, edited by Wright and Freund. Hakluyt Society, Second Series No. 103. London.

Wright, Roy 1974

The People of the Panther-A Long Erie Tale. In *Papers in Linguistics from the 1972 Conference on Iroquoian Research*:47–118. Michael K. Foster ed. National Museums of Canada, National Museum of Man Mercury Series, Ethnology Division Paper No. 10.

Wrong, George M. 1939
  The Long Journey to the Country of the Hurons. Gabriel Sagard, G.M.
  Wrong ed. The Champlain Society. Toronto.
Wroth, Lawrence C.
  1956
  The Champlain Map of 1616. John Carter Brown Library.
  1970
  The Voyages of Giovanni da Verrazano 1524-1528. Yale University
  Press. New Haven and London.
Zeller, A.G. 1962
  The Champlain-Iroquois Battle of 1615. Canastota Publishing Co. Inc.
  Canastota, New York.

INDEX

www.ingramcontent.com/pod-product-compliance
Lightning Source LLC
Chambersburg PA
CBHW050349110426
42812CB00008B/2410